Ripley's Believe It or Not!®

BIZARRE
COLLECTION

by Mary Packard

and the Editors of Ripley Entertainment Inc.

illustrations by Leanne Franson

SCHOLASTIC INC.

New York Toronto London Auckland Sydney
Mexico City New Delhi Hong Kong Buenos Aires

No part of this publication may be reproduced in whole or in part, or stored
in a retrieval system, or transmitted in any form or by any means, electronic,
mechanical, photocopying, recording, or otherwise, without written permission
of the publisher. For information regarding permission,
write to Scholastic Inc., Attention: Permissions Department,
557 Broadway, New York, NY 10012.

ISBN 0-439-64480-1

Ripley's Believe It or Not! Amazing Escapes, ISBN 0-439-31459-3,
Copyright © 2002 by Ripley Entertainment Inc. *Ripley's Believe It or Not!
Creepy Stuff*, ISBN 0-439-31457-7, Copyright © 2001 by Ripley Entertainment
Inc. *Ripley's Believe It or Not! Odd-inary People*, ISBN 0-439-31458-5,
Copyright © 2002 by Ripley Entertainment Inc. *Ripley's Believe It or Not! World's
Weirdest Critters*, ISBN 0-439-30617-5, Copyright © 2001 by Ripley
Entertainment Inc. All rights reserved. Ripley's Believe It or Not!, Believe It or
Not!, and Believe It! Are registered trademarks of Ripley Entertainment Inc.
Published by Scholastic Inc. SCHOLASTIC and associated logos are trademarks
and/or registered trademarks of Scholastic Inc.

12 11 10 9 8 7 6 5 4 3 2 1   4 5 6 7 8 9/0

Printed in the U.S.A.   40

First Scholastic printing, April 2004

Contents

Introduction

Ripley's Amazing, Unpredictable World

Think of the most famous celebrity you know. Perhaps the name of a sports figure, movie star, or recording artist comes to mind. That's how famous Robert Ripley was in his time. In the 1930s and 1940s, the Believe It or Not! craze was so popular that the phrase "There's one for Rip" was on everyone's lips whenever they saw or heard of an incredible person, animal, or event.

Although Ripley was a world traveler, he did not have to go far for inspiration. He received more than 3,500 letters per day—that's a million letters per year—from people who hoped that one of their experiences would be amazing enough to be featured in a Believe It or Not! cartoon.

Though his fame made it possible for Robert Ripley to live a life that was wealthy, ordered, and secure, he was well aware that all of his good luck could vanish in an instant. His cartoons were filled with stories that demonstrated the unpredictability of life—tales about people struck by lightning on sunny days, of shark attacks in shallow waters, and of tornadoes roaring through in the night.

Robert Ripley once tried to buy Paricutín, the volcano that was born in a Mexican cornfield (*see page 13 and color insert*).

Catastrophic disasters could occur at any time, especially in coastal regions and near fault lines, rivers, and volcanoes. The earth might swallow a city, a storm could level structures that had taken years to build, and rampaging floods or torrents of boiling lava might reduce a home to a mound of rubble or smoldering ash at any moment. Ripley marveled at such terrible events.

But even more astonishing to him were the stories of  the handful of survivors who, either by a stroke of good luck or by their own wits, squeaked through such disasters unharmed.

In *Amazing Escapes*, you'll find all kinds of thrilling stories of survival and heroism from the Ripley's archives. You can also test your "stranger than fiction" smarts by taking the No Way! quizzes and solving the Brain Buster in each chapter. Then you can try the special Pop Quiz at the end of the book and use the scorecard to rank your Ripley's knowledge.

So get ready! You're about to discover the amazing variety of people and animals that have endured every imaginable form of disaster—and a few unimaginable ones as well.

Believe It!®

CHAPTER 1 Nature's Fury

The survivors on the following pages have braved tornadoes, floods, lightning bolts, earthquakes, volcanic eruptions, and more.

Rude Awakening: On May 8, 1905, Oliver Ellwin of Lindsborg, Kansas, was sound asleep when a tornado whirled through his bedroom, swept his bed out of the house, and set the bed—and Ellwin— down unharmed in a field 500 feet away.

No Way!

The sound of the tornadoes in the movie *Twister* was made by a . . .

a. motorcycle in a tunnel.
b. pack of howling wolves.
c. subway train.
d. moaning camel.

Mud Bath: In 1997, Virginia Davidson took refuge in her bathtub and waited for a tornado to pass through her hometown of Jarrell, Texas. Before she knew it, she was swept

into the air, then set down in a field, right in the middle of a mud puddle. The bathtub was nowhere in sight.

Record Breaker: A tornado that struck Eldorado, Kansas, in 1958 sucked a woman through a window, carried her 60 feet through the air, and dropped her unharmed next to a broken record of "Stormy Weather." The tornado then collapsed her house like a pack of cards.

Grounded: In 1953, several children were playing together when a tornado struck Worcester, Massachusetts. Caught in the whirlwind of the tornado, the children were suddenly whisked into the air. Luckily, their mothers were around to grab hold of the kids and drag them back to earth.

Homespun: During a winter storm, a cottage in Malagash Point, Canada, was lifted from its foundation and set down a quarter mile away. Amazingly, everything inside remained intact—even the bottles on top of a kitchen cabinet.

No Way!

Benjamin Franklin once tried to break up a tornado by . . .

a. chasing it on horseback and lashing at it with a whip.
b. swinging at it with a lighted torch.
c. throwing chunks of dry ice at it.
d. spraying it with a hose.

At the End of Their Rope: In 1893, a hurricane smashed into South Carolina. With high winds blowing away anything in its path, many fast-thinking residents saved their lives by tying themselves to sturdy trees.

Moving Experience: In Pennsylvania, a 12-room house was carried away by the Johnstown flood on May 31, 1889. It was deposited two miles away on a foundation laid for a house that was being built from *identical* blueprints by the same contractor. William Thomas, owner of the property, bought the house and lived there for 43 years.

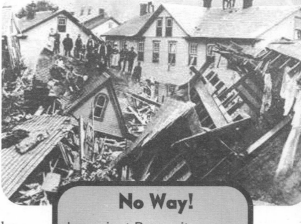

No Way!

In ancient Rome, it was believed that storms were caused by . . .

a. angering the god Jupiter.
b. wearing a soiled toga.
c. sporting a bad haircut.
d. speaking ill of one's mother-in-law.

Whew! On March 23, 1989, an asteroid larger than an aircraft carrier, traveling at a speed of about 46,000 miles per hour missed Earth by only six hours—or about 430,000 miles.

Up on the Rooftop:

In 1986, cows that were caught in a raging flood in Kansas climbed up on the rooftops of submerged houses and stayed there until they were rescued.

Windfall: On October 9, 1992, a tremendous bang sent Michelle Knapp of Peekskill, New York, scurrying from her house to investigate. What she found was puzzling at first. The trunk of her car had been badly smashed, but there was no other car in sight. When Knapp looked under the car, she found a

foul-smelling rock about the size of a watermelon. It was a meteorite that had crashed to Earth—and hit her car on the way. Knapp had paid only $100 for her 12-year-old Chevrolet Malibu, but collectors paid her $10,000 to get the car—and well over $50,000 to get the meteorite.

Lucky Strike: Eddie Robinson of Falmouth, Maine, was blind and partially deaf for nine years after suffering head injuries. In 1980, he was struck by lightning—and his vision and hearing were suddenly restored.

Branded! In 1968, a bolt of lightning tattooed a man with the initials of a doctor whom he had once robbed. Even more amazing, the man was revived by that very same doctor, who had just happened to be on the scene.

All Fired Up: After he was struck by lightning during a golf game, Anders B. Rasmussen of Denmark saw sparks shooting out of his fingers. To Rasmussen, the fact that he was still standing was a lucky sign, so he continued playing, hoping that his good luck would spill over to his game.

No Way!

A single bolt of lightning can produce 20,000 megawatts— enough energy to . . .

a. cool an entire sports arena.
b. fuel a space shuttle.
c. heat all the buildings in Manhattan.
d. supply all of Arizona with electricity.

Money to Burn:

In January of 1990, Canadians Don Wing and Jack Joneson got lost while skiing at Big Mountain Resort in Montana. They survived the extreme cold by burning dollar bills.

Suspended Sentence:

Mount Pelée, on the island of Martinique in the West Indies, erupted in 1902, killing more than 30,000 people and destroying the city of St. Pierre. Raoul Sarteret, a murderer who'd been sentenced to hang, was found in his dungeon-like jail cell, severely burned by the cloud of hot ash and gas but alive. Sarteret was later pardoned and went on to become a respected missionary.

The Candy Diet:

James Scott of Brisbane, Australia, was lost in a blizzard in the Himalayas. He survived for 43 days with only two candy bars to sustain him.

Hot Stuff!

For weeks there were tremors and rumbling sounds near the village of Paricutín, Mexico. Then on February 20, 1943, while a farmer named Dionisio Pulido was burning brush in his cornfield, the ground swelled up and cracked open.

Sulfurous gas and smoke poured out. By nightfall, the fissure was spitting hot cinders into the air. Within 24 hours, a cone had risen to 160 feet, and within a week, it had grown to more than 300 feet high. Named after the first of two villages it eventually covered with lava and ash, the new volcano, Paricutín, stood 1,100 feet above its base within a year.

No Way!

On August 27, 1883, the fiery volcanic explosion on Krakatoa, an island in Indonesia, was heard as far as 3,000 miles away. The first landing party to reach the ruined island found no survivors except for one . . .

a. ash-covered beetle.
b. red spider spinning its web.
c. cockroach crawling out of the ash.
d. dragonfly skimming an ashy puddle.

Whatever Works! When Mauna Loa erupted in 1880, an ocean of molten lava crept down the mountainside for six months, covering an area larger than the state of Rhode Island. The flow halted just one half mile before reaching the city of Hilo, more than 30 miles away! Many Hawaiians claimed that Hilo was spared because the Princess Kamahamena had thrown a lock of her hair into the fiery mass, hoping to calm it. When Mauna Loa erupted in 1935, the 23rd Bomb Squadron of the U.S. Army used twenty 600-pound bombs to change the direction of the lava flow and once again save Hilo from destruction.

Rocking and Rolling: With little warning, Mayon erupted on July 26, 2001. The Philippine volcano blasted out rocks the size of cars and sent them rolling down its slopes at speeds of 60 miles per hour. More than 40,000 villagers were forced to flee their homes. Ash showers known as "black rain" fell on towns as far as 31 miles away, turning morning into night. Though the eruption caused untold property damage, not a single life was lost.

What a Blast! For several months, Mount Saint Helens, a volcano in the state of Washington, had been rumbling and smoking. On May 18, 1990, geologists Keith and Dorothy Stoffel took off in their small plane to get a bird's-eye view of the crater. As they got close to the peak, there was a huge explosion. The pilot dived steeply to gain speed and they were able to outrun the huge cloud of hot ash and make it to safety with some of the finest photographs they'd ever taken.

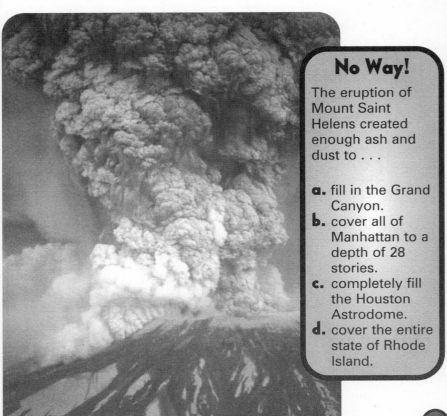

No Way!

The eruption of Mount Saint Helens created enough ash and dust to . . .

a. fill in the Grand Canyon.
b. cover all of Manhattan to a depth of 28 stories.
c. completely fill the Houston Astrodome.
d. cover the entire state of Rhode Island.

Slice of Life:

In December of 1920, earthquakes caused massive landslides in China. In one valley, three men survived when their farm split away from a cliff and traveled intact down the valley on a river of watery clay.

Jail Quakes:

Gabriel Maghalhaens (1609–1677), a Portuguese missionary to China, was arrested six times by Chinese authorities and received a death sentence all six times. On the night before each execution, however, an earthquake demolished his prison and set him free.

No Way!

Just before an earthquake struck the French Riviera in 1887 . . .

a. fish jumped out of the sea into boats.
b. all the cats began to meow at once.
c. horses refused to eat.
d. all the flowers wilted.

Fell Through the Crack:

When the largest North American earthquake ever recorded struck Alaska in 1964, Balas Ervin looked out a window and saw the earth suddenly shoot up 50 feet. The house had plunged to the bottom of a crevasse. Cans from the cupboards rained down on Ervin and a maid as they ran for the back door. Once

outside, they struggled to stay on their feet while the ground continued to shake. Finally, Ervin gave the maid a boost, and they clambered to the top of the fissure and escaped.

Road Trip:

In 1920, a poplar-lined highway in China, was carried intact for nearly a mile by a landslide. Even the birds' eggs in their nests were entirely unharmed.

A River Runs Backward: In 1811 and 1812, a series of major earthquakes struck New Madrid, Missouri, and played havoc with nature. In one place, both banks of the Mississippi River caved in, forcing the water to flow upstream.

On Shaky Ground: During the New Madrid, Missouri, earthquakes, huge cracks appeared in the ground. Noticing that they all ran in the same direction, the residents cut down trees and laid them at right angles to the fissures, When the earth trembled again, the people leaped onto the tree trunks, hoping the logs would serve as bridges across any new cracks and keep them safe.

No Shock Value: A Los Angeles earthquake in 1971 knocked out the seismograph—an instrument that records vibrations in the earth—in nearby Pasadena. It was here that Charles Richter (1900–1985) developed the Richter Scale, which measures earthquake intensity, in the early 1930s.

On the Ball:

In A.D. 132, a Chinese inventor named Chang Heng (A.D. 78–c. 142) devised the world's first instrument to detect earthquakes—even if the tremors were too far away to be felt. Heng's seismoscope was about eight feet tall and shaped like an urn. Around the outside of the urn were eight dragons, each holding a ball in its mouth and facing in a different direction. Below them were eight frogs. Whenever there was an earthquake, the inner workings of the urn triggered one of the dragons to drop its ball into the mouth of the frog below it, making a clanging noise. One day, a ball dropped, but no one nearby felt even the slightest tremor. It wasn't until several days later that a messenger came with word that an earthquake had indeed struck Lung-Hsi, which was located 400 miles away!

No Way!

About five earthquakes a year result in the loss of life. Yet, each year earthquakes that cause only mild tremors number more than . . .

a. one thousand.
b. five hundred.
c. one hundred.
d. one million.

Wave Good-bye: In 1946, a Hawaiian family survived a tsunami, an enormous sea wave, that lifted their house off the foundation, swept it 200 feet, and deposited it in a cane field—with the family's breakfast still simmering on the stove.

On Board: In 1868, Holoua, a resident of Kauai, Hawaii, whose home was swept out to sea by a tidal wave, saved himself by tearing a plank from the wall of the house and riding it back to shore. This event has been recorded in Honolulu as the highest wave ever surfed.

No Way!

After one city was leveled by a tidal wave in the fall of 1900, it was raised 17 feet above sea level and totally rebuilt. The name of this city is . . .

a. Charleston, South Carolina.
b. Galveston, Texas.
c. Provincetown, Massachusetts.
d. Miami, Florida.

Ripley believed that fact is stranger than fiction. Do you? Get ready to test your ability to tell a mind-blowing true tale from flat-out fiction!

The Ripley files are packed with true stories of daring deeds, unfortunate events, survivor skills, and close calls.

Each Believe It or Not! Brain Buster contains a group of four shockingly strange statements. In each group only **one** is **false**. Read each extraordinary entry and circle whether you **Believe It!** or **Not!** If you survive the challenge, take on the bonus question in each section and the bonus round at the end of the book. Then flip to the answer key, keep track of your score, and rate your skills. Got it? Good. Here goes . . .

Many athletes face extreme conditions on a regular basis—and completely by choice. Sports can be dangerous, but these adventurers came out on top. Only one of these extreme exploits is erroneous. Can you figure out which one?

a. Bicycle marathons are tough. So tough that Bobby Walthour was pronounced dead twice during one 60-day race. He recovered both times and peddled on.

Believe It!   **Not!**

b. Tao Berman was the first person to paddle a kayak over Johnston Canyon Waterfall in Alberta, Canada. Lined on both sides with jagged rock, the 98-foot drop is as high as a ten-story building.

Believe It!   Not!

c. Eighteen-year-old Regina Nair became a legend when she snowboarded down an icy peak near Mount Everest. Though she fell and broke her leg near the peak, Nair kept on and made it to the base, setting a new record.

Believe It!   Not!

d. Wim Hof of Holland dove into a hole carved through two feet of ice and swam 164 feet in one minute and six seconds. The kicker? The water was only two degrees warmer than the water that *Titanic* passengers froze in.

Believe It!   Not!

BONUS QUESTION

How did Wilma Rudolph of Clarksville, Tennessee, show the world that she's a survivor?

a. At 103, she was the oldest person ever to complete a marathon, running more than 26 miles.

b. She won three gold medals for running in the 1960 Olympics even though she had suffered from polio—a life-threatening illness—and worn leg braces as a child.

c. She went on to win a skateboarding competition just five minutes after she was struck by lightning.

Kids and animals get into scrapes sometimes. What's truly amazing is how often they get out of them.

No Yolk! In 1947, two-year-old baby Zsuzsie of Yugoslavia fell from a third-story window and landed in a basket of eggs carried by a passing peasant woman. The baby was not hurt— but the eggs got a little scrambled.

No Way!

In 1936, a cat was saved from a burning building when Blackie the firehouse dog . . .

a. chased it down a fire escape.
b. carried it down a ladder.
c. barked until it jumped into a blanket held by firefighters.
d. covered it with a fireproof blanket.

Rock-a-Bye Baby . . . In 1889, the flood that wiped out Johnstown, Pennsylvania, killed thousands. But it spared one five-month-old infant who sailed all the way to Pittsburgh, 75 miles away, on the floorboards of a ruined house.

. . . on the Treetop: After a tornado swept through Marshfield, Missouri, in April 1880, a baby girl was found sleeping peacefully in the branches of a tall elm tree.

Little Dropout: In 1992, Joshua Beatty, age two, of Southfield, Michigan, fell from a ninth-floor window. Incredibly, he survived unharmed. Why? Because the edge of his diaper got snagged on a bush, breaking his fall.

Bumper Sticker:

In 1993, two-year-old Allyson Hoary's dad got into his van to run an errand. Little did he know that Allyson was climbing on the back of the van as if it were a jungle gym at the time. He had already traveled six miles at 60 miles per hour when another motorist alerted him to the problem. When Hoary pulled over, he found Allyson clinging to the back of the van, shaken but uninjured.

No Way!

In 1993, five-year-old Paul Rosen of New York City lived after falling . . .

a. out of a taxi going 40 miles per hour.
b. off the Brooklyn Bridge.
c. from a seven-story apartment building.
d. through a grate onto the subway platform 25 feet below.

Lucky PJs: At the age of two, Albert Joseph of Miramar, Florida, fell into an unfenced canal bordering his backyard. He was saved from drowning when his pajamas filled with air, keeping little Albert's head above water.

Web Site: On July 13, 2001, a mama duck waddled up to a police officer in downtown Vancouver, Canada, and grabbed hold of his pant leg. Officer Ray Peterson pulled away from her, but she continued to quack and peck at him. Finally catching on, Peterson followed the duck to a sewer grate where he saw eight ducklings swimming in the water below. A tow truck was called, the heavy metal grate was lifted, and the mama's babies were pulled to safety in a colander.

Buried Alive: Glenda Stevens was heartbroken when her small black dog, Sweetie, was hit by a mail truck. She listened carefully for a heartbeat. When she didn't hear one, she tearfully buried her beloved pet in her backyard. Hours later, Stevens saw Sweetie's hind legs sticking out of the ground. Sweetie, who wasn't dead after all, was digging herself out!

Not Too Sharp: In 1993, Tyro, a three-month-old Labrador retriever puppy in British Columbia, Canada, made a full recovery after swallowing a nine-inch knife!

Blackout: In 1997, Sparky, a black cat in East Corinth, Maine, was trapped for three days on top of a telephone pole. The cat survived thunderstorms and a jolt from a 7,500-volt power line that had left 1,000 homes without electricity.

No Way!

Nathan King, age 12, of Helena, Montana, made a full recovery after an accident on March 8, 2000, in which he . . .

a. lunged for a football and landed on a pencil that pierced his heart.
b. fell from a plane without a parachute.
c. fell off a deck into an empty swimming pool.
d. stumbled off a stage and fell into the orchestra pit.

Eggs-tremely Resourceful: A red hen owned by J. D. Rucker was trapped in a crate when a tornado devastated the town of Gainesville, Georgia. It was rescued 47 days later on May 22, 1936. Noticeably thinner, it had survived by eating its own eggs.

Barn-Sided: In 1998, Kate Wilson of London, England, got out of her car, leaving her two dogs inside. The romping canines accidentally released the emergency brake—and took an unexpected joyride that lasted until they crashed into the side of a barn.

Go Fly a Kite: Eight-year-old Deandra Anrig was flying her brand-new 12-foot-wide kite at Shoreline Park in Mountain View, California, when all of a sudden, a twin-engine plane caught the kite's nylon line. The plane lifted the little girl off the ground and carried her 100 feet before she let go— just in time to avoid smashing into a very large tree.

Taken by Storm:

In 1908, 18-month-old Renée Nivernas of France was kidnapped and held for ransom aboard a boat. When a storm blew up, the boat sank and all eight kidnappers drowned. But Renée, asleep in a packing-case cradle, floated ashore unharmed.

No Way!

In 1993, eight-year-old Nicole Bernier of Willington, Connecticut, survived after . . .

a. falling out the window of her third-floor bedroom.
b. spending two days beneath an avalanche.
c. a freight train passed over her body.
d. she fell to the bottom of the Grand Canyon.

Way Down Under: In 1990, nine-month-old Sara Gillies, of Perth, Australia, survived after her baby carriage was hit and crushed by an oncoming train.

Trial by Fire: In 1947, when Albert Lametta was 12 years old, he climbed to the top of an electrical tower, touched a 6,600-volt wire, and fell 60 feet. Though badly burned, he eventually made a full recovery.

Fish Tale: In July of 1999, a goldfish was scooped from a pond by a heron and dropped down a chimney in Northampton, England—where it bounced off the hot coals before it was rescued and placed in a bowl of water.

Where's Toto? In 1994, a tornado in Le Mars, Iowa, picked up a doghouse with a dog inside and set it down several blocks away without harming the dog in any way.

No Way!

On September 8, 1860, 297 lives were lost when the *Lady Elgin* sank in Lake Michigan. One little boy, Charles Beverung, saved himself by . . .

a. clinging to the coffin of a dead man.
b. using his drum as a life raft.
c. jumping off the deck onto a steamer trunk.
d. treading water for 14 hours.

Home Wrecker: Five-month-old James Clark of West Bend, Wisconsin, was sound asleep when a tornado blew his room apart and dropped him outside on the sidewalk. The baby was not injured!

Bolt Out of the Blue: On a beautiful sunny day in June 2001, a Little Leaguer in North Carolina was covering third base when a sudden storm blew in. There was a sound like a cannon shot, and the boy was struck by a bolt of lightning. Luckily, he was revived on the field and rushed to the hospital, where he was treated for burns.

No Way!

In 1960, seven-year-old Roger Woodward became the only person ever to survive . . .

a. falling off the Empire State Building.
b. being attacked by a bear in Yosemite National Park.
c. accidentally going over Niagara Falls.
d. falling off the Golden Gate Bridge.

Brain Buster

Life is filled with narrow escapes and near misses—some more dramatic than others. Three of the following escapes are 100% accurate, but one is totally made up. Can you pick out the fiction?

a. In 1997, Nigel Etherington of Perth, Australia, rescued a baby kangaroo. The kangeroo later returned the favor when it woke Etherington up during a fire by banging its tail on a door.

Believe It!   **Not!**

b. In 1775, three women in a ruined stable in Stura Valley, Italy, survived being buried by a 60-foot-deep avalanche of snow. But they didn't escape unscathed. When the women were rescued, one had lost all of her hair and another could no longer speak.

Believe It!   **Not!**

c. The small South American island of Tristan da Cunha is the only place on Earth that escaped the 1918 Spanish influenza—a fast-spreading disease that killed more than 21 million people all over the world.

Believe It!   **Not!**

d. In July 2000, a 12-year-old girl accidentally fell into a raging river near her family's home and was quickly swept downstream by the current. The girl was seconds away from crashing into a giant boulder when a female black bear jumped into the water, swam the girl to shore, and left her on the ground unharmed.

Believe It!   **Not!**

• •

BONUS QUESTION

How did King Malcolm McAnmore of Scotland's bodyguard keep 20 assassins from killing the king?

a. By triggering an avalanche. The bodyguard fired off a cannon on the roof of the castle, which sent 40 tons of snow and ice tumbling onto the assassins below.

b. By holding the castle door closed with just one arm and preventing the assassins from getting in.

c. By firing a cannon into the moat surrounding the castle. The water rose, drowning a few of the assassins and distracting the others long enough for the bodyguard and the king to sneak out of the castle through a secret underground passage.

Transportation mishaps can be deadly—one wrong move, and you're history. What's unbelievable is that so many people survive!

Crushing Experience:

In 1994, a truck in Arenys de Mar, Spain, was hit by a car, pushed onto a railroad track, and crushed by an oncoming train. The truck's driver and passenger walked away from the wreck with only minor injuries.

No Way!

In 1999, British actress Sara Donohue survived a crash at 100 miles per hour while racing her . . .

a. boat.
b. motorcycle.
c. Formula 1 race car.
d. snowmobile.

Stone-Walled: A biplane caught in a storm flew 275 miles from Colorado to Oklahoma with 4,700 holes in its wings and fuselage. What made so many holes? Hailstones the size of baseballs!

The Whole Scoop:

In 1955, the drivers of two cars that collided in Santa Barbara, California, walked away uninjured. One was named Coffey and the other Pott, but the police found no *grounds* on which to hold either driver.

No Way!

The ship *Californian* was only five miles away from the sinking *Titanic*, but instead of coming to its aid, the captain calmly went to sleep after . . .

a. turning off the ship's radio and missing the SOS call.

b. misreading a chart and thinking the *Titanic* was 500 miles away.

c. his radio operator fell asleep and missed the call for help.

d. he mistook the *Titanic*'s emergency flares for fireworks.

Take a Dive:

After colliding with another skydiver near Phoenix, Arizona, in April 1987, Debbie Williams was knocked unconscious. It's a good thing Gregory Robertson was the next person to jump. He caught up to her by going into a 200-mile-per-hour free fall and opened her parachute just seconds before she would have struck the ground.

Busch-Whacked:

In 1953, a car driven by Clayton Busch was hit by two trains at the same time. Busch was found standing close to the tracks, still clutching the car's steering wheel.

Under-Tow: Because motorists' cars frequently plunge into Amsterdam's many canals, drivers in the city are given courses in how to get themselves out of automobiles that are submerged in water.

Charmed Life: Frank Tower swam away from three major shipwrecks: the *Titanic* in 1912, the *Empress of Ireland* in 1914, and the *Lusitania* in 1915.

On the Beam: During a violent storm in the 19th century, Captain Benjamin Webster was swept overboard from the *Isaac Johnson* at the same time that a load of lumber on deck was cut loose. The captain landed on one of the beams. A moment later, a giant wave hurled that *one* board back onto the ship's deck with the captain safely astride it.

Springing to Life: After the shipwrecked *Lara* was destroyed by fire in 1881, its crew drifted for 23 days in three lifeboats off the coast of Mexico. Several crewmen were unconscious from thirst. But they were saved when the captain noticed that the water beneath their boats had changed color from blue to green as they drifted over a freshwater spring. The fresh water revived them, and the entire crew reached Mexico safely.

No Way!

A jetliner was delayed in Juneau, Alaska, for an hour after a midair mishap caused by . . .

a. hailstones that damaged the fuselage.
b. a seagull that flew into the engine.
c. a salmon (that was dropped by an eagle) crashing through the windshield.
d. a family of geese that hitched a ride on a wing.

One Foggy Night: On July 25, 1956, two passenger ships, the *Andrea Doria* and the *MV Stockholm* crashed in the North Atlantic near Nantucket, Massachusetts. Survivors remember feeling a massive jolt and hearing the sickening noise of crunching metal. Though 46 passengers died that foggy night, the incident remains one of the most amazing rescues in the history of maritime disasters. The rest of the 1,654 passengers were pulled to safety aboard the five ships that answered the distress call. Coincidentally, one of the survivors, Ruby MacKenzie, had just finished reading *A Night to Remember,* a novel about the sinking of the *Titanic.*

The Right Wavelength:

In May 1945, Lieutenant Commander Robert W. Goehring was swept off his ship by a mountainous wave during a storm. Just when he thought that all was lost, another giant wave tossed him back on board to safety.

Stress Test: On July 19, 2001, a teenager was passing her driving test with flying colors—until she attempted to parallel park. Somehow she lost control of the car, smashed into four other cars, then spun around and hit two more. The driving instructor was treated for shock, and the teen and a woman who was standing between two of the cars had minor injuries, but no one was seriously hurt.

No Way!

In Nantucket, Massachusetts, lumber salvaged from shipwrecks was used to build a . . .

a. tavern.
b. windmill.
c. captain's home.
d. lighthouse.

In a Tailspin: On a routine passenger flight over Czechoslovakia in 1972, flight attendant Vesna Vulovic was inside the plane's tail when the plane exploded. She survived being thrown 33,000 feet to the ground.

Narrow Escape: In 1993, all 163 passengers on an Air India flight that crashed and landed *upside down* walked away from the wreckage before the plane burst into flames.

Icebound: When their ship, the *Endurance,* became icebound in 1914, Ernest Shackleton and his entire 27-man crew survived 19 months of brutal weather and dangerous travel across Antartica's ice and frigid waters.

Tall Tail: Captain J. H. Hedley of Chicago, Illinois, fell out of a plane nearly three miles up in the air on January 6, 1918. Incredibly, just as the plane was making a steep vertical dive in line with his own fall, Hedley landed on the tail. He made it to the ground, shaken but uninjured.

All Clogged Up: When ash from a volanic eruption in Alaska clogged and stalled the engines of a Dutch passenger plane in 1989, the airliner went into a dive and plunged two miles. To the relief of everyone aboard, the pilots were able to get the engines started again and safely land the plane.

No Way!

After the *Titanic* sank, most newspapers carried a headline announcing that . . .

a. there were no survivors.
b. everyone had been rescued.
c. the captain had been saved.
d. the ship was being towed to shore.

Piggyback Landing: In December of 1999, flight instructor Alan Vangee was flying with student Barbara Yeninas in a Cessna 152 when a Piper Cadet airplane cleared to land on the same runway wedged itself on top of their plane. Vangee successfully landed the two planes—and no one was hurt.

No Way!

In a study of over 260 voice-recorder tapes removed from airplanes involved in accidents since 1966, 80 percent revealed that during the last half hour of flight, one of the pilots was . . .

a. phoning his wife.
b. laughing at a joke.
c. whistling.
d. gossiping with a flight attendant.

Ripley's Believe It or Not! Brain Buster

The Ripley's files are filled with some very bizarre accounts of near tragedy. Which of these amazing escapes is completely false?

a. In 1989, Buster Bradshaw of Haverford, Pennsylvania, survived the crash of his private plane by holding a wheel of Swiss cheese over his face. The soft cheese cushioned the impact and prevented Bradshaw from suffering severe injuries to the head.

Believe It!　　　　**Not!**

b. In 1985, Eric Villet of Orléans, France, was pronounced officially dead after doctors unsuccessfully tried to revive him with heart massage and oxygen. Shockingly, he started breathing on his own three days later—while lying in the morgue!

Believe It!　　　　**Not!**

c. During the World Extreme Skiing Championship in 1992, Garret Bartelt tumbled down the mountain's steepest slope without protective gear. It was the longest fall in professional skiing history—but Bartelt survived with only minor injuries and was back on the slopes competing in another championship two years later.

Believe It!　　　　**Not!**

d. In the 1930s, Douglas Ellis of Cleveland, Ohio, came in contact with a 22,000-volt line. Although 60 square inches of his skull were removed, Ellis survived.

Believe It!　　　　**Not!**

BONUS QUESTION

How did Admiral Richard E. Byrd survive temperatures of 83°F *below* zero while spending six months in Antarctica?

a. By living in a 9-by-13-foot shack beneath the snow.

b. By burning the lining of his shoes to keep warm.

c. By exercising for 14 hours a day to keep his body temperature high.

4 Nice Saves

Should you find yourself in a really tight spot, it's nice to know that there just might be someone brave enough to come to the rescue.

Track Star: On June 25, 1913, a locomotive on its way to Holland plunged over the side of a bridge. The engine, on the brink of falling, would have exploded if it were not for the engineer, who at great risk to himself climbed down through the engine to put out the fire in the furnace.

No Way!

A woman who fell down and lost consciousness was saved when a family pet went straight to her sister's house and tapped on the window. The pet was a . . .

a. goat.
b. collie.
c. canary.
d. pig.

In the Driver's Seat: In December of 1991, after the driver of his school bus blacked out, 12-year-old Kenny Perrone of Dunellon, Florida, came to the rescue. Quickly taking control of the wheel, he guided the vehicle to safety, saving all 33 kids on board.

Hangin' Eight: After a yacht capsized in rough waters off Newport Beach, California, in 1925, Hawaiian surfer Duke Kahanamoku single-handedly saved the lives of eight passengers by using his surfboard to carry them to shore.

Human Anchor: On October 28, 1844, Margaret Whyte of Aberdour, Scotland, was the only person onshore when the sailing ship *William Hope* was driven into the rocks by a raging storm. Whyte signaled the crew to throw her a line. With no tree or post available, she tied the rope around her waist, dug her heels into the sand, and held the line taut against the pull of the tossing vessel while its entire crew of 12 came ashore one by one.

No Way!

On September 22, 1938, hundreds of acres of valuable land in the town of Stony Point, New York, were saved from flooding by . . .

a. hundreds of trees felled by Eagle Scouts to divert the flow of water.
b. thousands of sandbags filled by townspeople.
c. the dams built by 60 beaver colonies.
d. tons of sludge dumped by the Coast Guard.

Critter Comfort: When five-year-old Levan Merritt fell 20 feet into a gorilla compound at England's Jersey Zoo, a gorilla named Jambo protected the injured boy by keeping the other gorillas away. Jambo then comforted the boy until human help could arrive.

Human Bus Stop: In December of 1996, bus driver Hamdija Osmana of Yugoslavia kept his bus from rolling over a cliff—with 30 passengers inside—by jamming his legs under a wheel and stopping the vehicle. He saved the lives of all 30 passengers.

Four to the Rescue: If it weren't for four brave siblings, three of their neighbors might have died in the fire that blazed through their Freeport, New York, home on July 16, 2001. Felicia Pettus was trapped in an upstairs room with her two young children, Alexis and Kyra. Responding to her screams, 14-year-old Robert Hester and 16-year-old Jacob ran into the house, braving smoke and rising flames. But when they got upstairs, they couldn't get the door open. The boys ran back outside, where their 12-year-old sister, Jaquana, and 17-year-old stepbrother, Nathaniel Richardson, were shouting encouragement. Urging Pettus to jump, the siblings caught Alexis, then her mother. Robert then ran back into the house to get Kyra. He emerged holding his shirt over his head with one arm and the toddler in the other. When firefighters arrived at the scene, they had nothing but praise for this family of young heroes.

No Way!

Count Felix von Luckener, a German cabin boy aboard the *Noibe,* fell overboard, but was kept afloat and saved from drowning by . . .

a. a sea turtle.
b. an albatross.
c. a dolphin.
d. a manatee.

Warm and Fuzzy Heating Pad:

Accompanied by his dog Sheena, three-year-old Justin Pasero of Susanville, California, wandered away into the Sierra Nevada Mountains and spent the night inside a hollow log. He was kept from freezing to death by Sheena, who kept Justin warm with her own body.

This Little Piggy Played Dead:

In Beaver Falls, Pennsylvania, a potbelly pig named Lulu saved the life of her owner. Jo Altsman was home alone the morning she suffered a massive heart attack. When she fell to the floor, Lulu lay her head on Altsman's chest and cried real tears. Then the brave pig sprang into action. Lulu squeezed herself through the doggie door, which was only one foot wide. Then she ran into the road where she lay down and played dead to get someone's attention. Minutes later, a young man stopped. Lulu got up and led the man to the trailer. When he knocked on the door, Altsman answered faintly, "Call 911." At the hospital, doctors credited Lulu with saving Altsman's life.

Up in Arms: When fire ravaged a Milwaukee hotel in 1883, firefighter Van Haag fought the flames to save General Tom Thumb and his wife. Thumb, who was only three feet four inches tall, was a world-famous performer who worked for showman P. T. Barnum.

No Way!

During the 1800s, shipwrecked sailors sent lifelines to rescuers on shore by attaching them to . . .

a. seagulls.
b. kites.
c. fishing poles.
d. dolphins.

Pod Squad: In 1991, a pod of dolphins protected a group of shipwrecked sailors from circling sharks off the coast of Florida.

Did Swimmingly: Nellie O'Donnell had never learned to swim. But in June of 1904, she saw an excursion boat, the *General Slocum,* sinking in New York's East River. Hundreds of people were about to drown. With no thought for her own safety, O'Donnell jumped into the water and saved ten lives before she collapsed with exhaustion.

In a Heartbeat: In June 2001, a pet hamster was overcome by smoke after a washer exploded and started a fire in Nottingham, England. A firefighter saved the hamster's life by giving him oxygen and a one-finger heart massage.

Nice Catch!
Nine-year-old Joey Rains of Newark, California, caught 17-month-old Sara Wolf when she fell from an open second-story window of her apartment building. Neither was hurt.

Oh, Deer!

In 1992, Gene Chaffin of Encinitas, California, rescued a pregnant doe after she was struck by a car. He delivered her two fawns and saved one of them by giving it mouth-to-mouth resuscitation.

Human Cork: In January of 1870, Captain Thomas A. Scott brought his tugboat alongside a sinking ferryboat carrying hundreds of passengers in New York's North River. Boarding the ferry, Scott used his body to plug a hole at the waterline of the listing boat. His arm, which protruded through the hole, was severely lacerated by ice, but everyone aboard the vessel was saved.

No Way!

A short circuit caused a fire in the home of James A. Dewitt, who was saved when . . .

a. the short circuit set off the doorbell, jarring him awake.
b. his parrot kept squawking, "Get up, get up!"
c. a pipe burst and put out the fire.
d. his ferret crawled up his pajama leg and woke him up.

Canine Lifeline: On December 10, 1919, the S.S. *Ethie,* a 414-ton steamship, ran aground off Newfoundland, Canada, in a violent storm. With the ship breaking up in heavy seas, the captain couldn't launch the lifeboats, and none of the crew dared swim ashore with a lifeline. But all was not lost. A Newfoundland dog gripped the lifeline in his teeth and swam to the beach, where a bystander secured the line and all 92 passengers and crew were pulled to safety.

No Way!

In 1997, Gail Brooks's boyfriend was attacked by a shark. She saved his life by . . .

a. pouring sand into the wound to soak up the blood.

b. making a tourniquet out of her bathing suit strap.

c. tying off a bleeding artery with dental floss.

d. freezing the wound with ice from the cooler.

People will do the oddest things no matter how dangerous, terrifying, or life-threatening their actions may be. See if you can tell which one of these death-defying feats are false.

a. Tim Cridland takes performance art to a new height. Using only pain-deadening meditation, he lies down on a bed of nails and lets a 3,000-pound vehicle drive over him, surviving despite the huge weight and sharp nails.
Believe It!   **Not!**

b. Sixteen-year-old Janice Stellman dived from a 500-foot cliff into the ocean off the coast of New Zealand in 1997 "just for fun." Stellman survived despite blacking out halfway down.
Believe It!   **Not!**

c. In 1837, to demonstrate the power of meditation, yogi Haridas put himself into a trance, then allowed assistants to fill his ears, nose, and mouth with wax. The assistants went on to wrap him in a blanket and bury him alive. Forty days later, he was dug up, looking a little on the skinny side but perfectly healthy.
Believe It!   **Not!**

d. Smokey Harris had his nose broken seven times, his jaw broken four times, his ribs broken 14 times, both knees broken, half a foot amputated, and 100 operations on his head—all for the sake of playing hockey. What dedication!
Believe It!   **Not!**

BONUS QUESTION

Maddie Mix of Baton Rouge, Louisiana, is one lucky woman. She was driving in her car when nearly 10,000 bees attacked. How did she escape?

a. She happened to be eating a peanut butter and honey sandwich, which she used to distract the hungry bees while she carefully pulled over and slipped out of the car.

b. She drove her car through the wall of a nearby molasses silo, causing the sticky liquid to flow into the car and smother the bees.

c. She drove into a car wash where she was rescued by a beekeeper who just happened to be washing his car at the time.

If you think the escapes in the previous pages are unbelievable, wait until you read these!

Snake Medicine: In 1996, Valentin Grimald of Texas was bitten by a coral snake. He killed the poisonous reptile by biting off its head, then used its body as a tourniquet to stop the poison from spreading throughout his body, and saved his own life.

No Way!

W. V. Meadows of West Point, Georgia, was shot in the eye at the battle of Vicksburg on July 1, 1863. Fifty-eight years later, he . . .

a. regained sight in that eye.
b. coughed up the bullet.
c. wrote and sang "Eyewitness," a song about the Civil War.
d. accidentally shot himself in the other eye.

Saved by the Dill: In 1994, four restaurant employees in Jeffersonville, Indiana, were locked in a freezer by robbers, who then set fire to the building in an effort to destroy evidence. The fire was contained, however, when the blaze reached a plastic bucket of pickles. The bucket melted, the pickle juice extinguished the flames, and the victims were saved.

Tongue-Tied: Fourteen-year-old Duane Della of Altoona, Pennsylvania, reached out to grab his two-year-old niece who was climbing into the basement freezer. Unfortunately, Duane lost his balance and toppled in, landing face-first. When he opened his mouth to yell for help, his tongue instantly stuck fast to the bottom of the freezer. Fortunately, firefighters were able to loosen his tongue (from the freezer!) and pull him out.

Whale of a Story: In 1891, James Bartley, a 36-year-old seaman on the British whaler *Star of the East,* was swallowed by a sperm whale. Bartley's crewmates quickly harpooned the whale, badly injuring it. The next day, the whale was found dead, floating on the surface. After hauling it aboard and slicing it open, the crew found Bartley, unconscious but still breathing, in the whale's stomach. He was delirious for days but recovered to 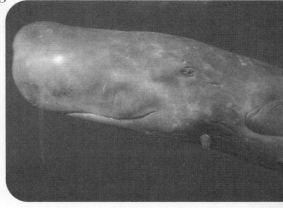 describe his ordeal. Before passing out, Bartley remembered seeing "a big ribbed canopy of light pink and white" above him, "a wall of soft flesh surrounding him and hemming him in," and then finding himself inside a water-filled sack among fish, some of which were still alive.

Snail's Pace: in 1996, a train on the Casablanca-Fez railroad line in Morocco slipped off the rails after a horde of snails slimed the tracks!

No Way!

In 1930, Phineas P. Gage of Cavendish, Vermont, survived an explosion that drove a 13-pound iron bar through his . . .

a. brain.
b. lungs.
c. heart.
d. stomach.

Blasted Sky-High: A blast of air pressure in 1905 blew Richard Creedon, a New York City sandhog (a person who works on tunnels for city waterlines), out of an East River tunnel shaft. Unhurt after flying through 27 feet of silt and water into the air, Creedon said, "Before I came down, I had a fine view of the city."

Cushy Landing: On January 6, 1983, Keung Ng of Boston, Massachusetts, was asleep in his fourth-floor apartment when the building was destroyed by an explosion. Incredibly, Ng survived. Still in his bed, he fell down three flights to where the ground floor used to be and landed on a pile of debris. Then Ng got up and walked away.

Horse Nonsense:

During the Civil War, southern raiders kidnapped two slaves, a mother and her infant son, in Missouri. Mary disappeared, but her son was found and ransomed by his master for a valuable racehorse. Moses Carver then adopted the baby, who grew up to be the distinguished scientist and dean of Tuskegee Institute, George Washington Carver.

Such a Headache:

In 1867, William Thompson of Omaha, Nebraska, was shot by Native Americans of the Cheyenne tribe. Thinking he was dead, they removed part of his scalp. Imagine their surprise when Thompson regained consciousness, grabbed his scalp, and ran. He later donated the scalp to the Omaha Public Library.

No Way!

Sarah Ann Henley survived falling 250 feet from the Clifton Suspension Bridge in England when . . .

a. her petticoat opened like a parachute.

b. an eagle swooped down and caught her dress in its beak.

c. she landed in the swimming pool of a yacht.

d. her dress caught on a steel girder.

Instant Weight Loss: Imprisoned for 100 days in the Tower of London, Sir Thomas Overbury (1581–1613) survived being fed a diet of nitric acid, hemlock, and ground diamonds.

Don't Mess with Me! In 1992, while diving off Catalina Island in California, Norma Hansen survived an attack by a great white shark by kicking its teeth out with her steel-toed boots.

Sealed with a Kiss: Downy Ferrer of Laguna Hills, California, had to be rescued by paramedics after she kissed her pet turtle. Why? Because it clamped onto her upper lip and wouldn't let go!

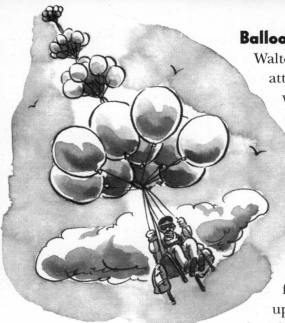

Balloonatic: In 1982, Larry Walters of California attached more than 40 weather balloons to his lawn chair and filled them with helium. He packed a soda, a two-way radio, and a pellet gun, then strapped himself to the chair. The rope holding the chair down was cut free—and Walters shot up three miles into the sky, where he drifted for hours before he got chilly, shot some of the balloons with his pellet gun, and drifted back to Earth.

No Way!

In 1728, Margaret Dickson was already in her coffin when she came back to life after being . . .

a. hanged for murder.
b. run over by a stagecoach.
c. scalped.
d. thrown from her horse.

On the Fly: Angel Santana of New York City escaped unharmed when a robber's bullet bounced off his pant zipper.

Human Pipe Cleaner: In 1989, William Lamm of Vero Beach, California, escaped unhurt after he was sucked into a water intake pipe and traveled through it for 1,500 feet at 50 miles per hour.

Major Revival: In 1997, a Norwegian fisherman, Jan Egil Refsdahl, fell overboard in the North Atlantic Ocean. His heart stopped for four hours and his body temperature fell to 77°F, yet he completely recovered.

Holy Smokestack! While repairing a high smokestack in Philadelphia, Pennsylvania, Dave Biddle fell ten stories, smashed through a concrete roof, and landed on a metal catwalk. His only injury was a broken ankle.

Had a Blast! A man from Kansas City, Missouri, decided to celebrate the Fourth of July with his friends. His neighbors were disturbed by the fireworks, so they

called the police. Eager to hide the evidence, someone stashed the fireworks in the oven—and everyone forgot about them. Later, the man decided to bake some lasagna. When he turned the oven on, a huge explosion blew the kitchen to bits. Luckily, no one was hurt except for minor injuries caused by flying glass.

The Sky Is Falling!

Joanne and Mahlon Donovan of Derry, New Hampshire, were asleep in their home when a speeding car hit a hill, became airborne, and crashed into the Donovans' bedroom. The couple only survived because the car landed with one end propped up on a dresser, clearing their bed by a mere 12 inches.

No Way!

Old Man's Day is celebrated on October 2 in Hertfordshire, England, to commemorate the survival of Matthew Hall, a 16th-century farmer, who. . .

a. was trampled by a herd of stampeding dairy cows.

b. was revived when pallbearers accidentally dropped his coffin on the road.

c. rescued a family of ten from a burning farmhouse.

d. was struck by lightning on his 90th birthday.

Board to Death: In October 1991, John Ferreira of California survived a great white shark attack when he choked the shark by jamming his surfboard into its jaws.

A Lot at Stake: In the mid-1990s, Neil Pearson fell and impaled himself on a metal pipe used as a plant stake. The pipe went into his armpit, through his body, and out through his neck below his ear. X rays revealed that the stake missed his carotid artery and every vital organ in its path. Doctors say that if this freak accident were a medical procedure, it would have been deemed too risky. All Pearson needed was five stitches to close up the wound. He was released from the hospital the same day!

Jawbreaker: In 1963, Rodney Fox survived an attack by a 1,200-pound great white shark despite having sustained a wound in his side that required 462 stitches.

No Way!

When Wess Martin, foreman of a California ice plant, was accidentally locked in the company's icebox, he kept from freezing to death by . . .

a. doing 5,000 jumping jacks.
b. break dancing.
c. meditating.
d. pushing blocks of ice around.

Left a Bad Taste: In 1771, the *Boston Post* reported that an American harpooner named Jenkins was swallowed by a sperm whale when it snapped his whale boat in two with one bite. Jenkins disappeared into the huge jaws but must have disagreed with the whale—it spat him out right away. Jenkins was not hurt.

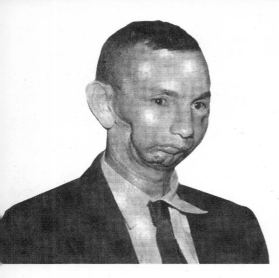

Bulletproof Man: On March 18, 1915, Wenseslao Moguel of Mérida, Mexico, survived execution by a firing squad—even after the final bullet was fired at close range to ensure a quick death.

All Fall Down! On July 17, 1990, Kelli Harrison and David Darrington of Australia had no sooner crossed London Bridge, a double arch in a seaside cliff caused by erosion, when they heard an enormous splash. When they looked back, they saw that the part of the land they'd just walked on had disappeared. The centuries-old arch had crumbled into the sea. Had the pair crossed 30 seconds later, they would have perished. Thankful to have survived their very close call, Harrison and Darrington were flown to safety by a police helicopter.

No Way!

Moments after being shot in the chest by a would-be assassin, this United States president delivered a one-hour speech. His name was . . .

a. Theodore Roosevelt.
b. William Howard Taft.
c. Rutherford B. Hayes.
d. Thomas Jefferson.

The Human Cannonball:

In 1782, an Indian holy man named Aruna, who angered the sultan of Mysore, was twice stuffed into a cannon and fired into the air. He survived both times. The first time, he was blown 800 feet and landed on the soft canopy atop an elephant. The second time, he fell without a scratch onto the thatched roof of a hut.

What a Crock! In the late 1960s, when a crocodile clamped down on the leg of a citizen of Tamative, Madagascar, the man grabbed hold of the crocodile's leg and won his freedom and his life after an hour-long tug-of-war.

Biting the Bull: When a pit bull clamped its vicelike jaws around the head of a young Scottish terrier on June 16, 2001, the terrier's owner, 73-year-old Margaret Hargrove of Tallahassee, Florida, sprang into action. She tried to pry open the pit bull's jaws but was unsuccessful. Not one to give up easily, Hargrove got down on her knees and bit the dog in the neck! The pit bull let go immediately, then bit Hargrove on the arm. Both owner and terrier needed stitches to close up their wounds.

No Way!

While attempting to parachute into Sumatra in 1997, Sergeant Cyril Jones crashed into the forest and was suspended in the trees for 12 days. He survived by eating . . .

a. all different kinds of bugs.
b. fruit brought to him by a monkey.
c. leaves he cut off with his pocketknife.
d. tree frogs and lizards.

You know what you have to do—find the fiction!

a. In 1997, Hurricane Pauline saved the lives of three people who had been lost at sea off the coast of Mexico for 15 days. The high winds swept them all safely back to shore!

Believe It!   Not!

b. During the Middle Ages, French troops were spared an attack by the army of England's Edward III when 1,000 knights were killed by a rain of deadly hail.

Believe It!   Not!

c. While taking part in a 1999 gliding exhibition at a local festival in Missouri, two pilots steered their planes into a gigantic thundercloud hoping the winds would boost them higher. No such luck! When the storm threatened to destroy their planes, the pilots jumped out into an updraft that kept them airborne long enough for a third plane to fly in and rescue them.

Believe It!   Not!

d. During World War II, the United States Navy began studying ways of steering typhoons toward enemy ships. How did the Navy come up with the idea? Three of its own destroyers and nearly 800 men were lost in a typhoon in the Philippines on December 17, 1944.

Believe It!   Not!

BONUS QUESTION

What role did the weather play in Christopher Columbus's voyage to the Americas?

a. Steady winds had been blowing the *Niña*, the *Pinta*, and the *Santa Maria* westward on their journey for so many days, the sailors were afraid the winds would never reverse and they'd never get home. But as the crews were plotting mutiny, the heavy waves from a powerful hurricane miles away convinced them there would be enough wind to get the ships back to Spain after their voyage of discovery was over. They abandoned their plans to take over the ships. Columbus survived and the fleet sailed onward to the Americas.

b. For years, there had been reports of sunken treasure only 100 miles off Columbus's course. Millions of dollars worth of gold and silver were believed to be aboard a Spanish armada that disappeared in a fierce cyclone in 1415. The crew wanted to look for the treasure when a new cyclone kicked up, almost capsizing the *Pinta* and taking the lives of several crew members. The surviving sailors decided to forget about the treasure and sail on.

c. The fleet was forced to ride out a dangerous hurricane for hours. When the winds finally died down, the crew realized the ships had been blown 500 miles closer to the land mass that would later be called the Americas.

It's not over yet. How many true rescues, survivor stories, and amazing escapes do you remember? Ready to find out? Circle your answers, and give yourself five points for each question you answer correctly.

1. In March 1989, Earth had a near miss with an asteroid the size of an aircraft carrier traveling at a speed of about 46,000 miles per hour. The extraterrestrial wrecking ball missed Earth by just six hours.

Believe It!   **Not!**

2. Which of the following was *not* caused by the forces of nature?

a. A tornado changed the direction that water swirls in a toilet.

b. A volcano turned morning into night.

c. An earthquake forced part of the Mississippi River to flow upstream.

3. Which of the following was *not* caused by a bolt of lightning?

a. Sparks shot out of one man's fingers.

b. One man's body became magnetized, and large metal objects stuck to his limbs for the next six months.

c. One man's vision and hearing were suddenly restored after nine years of being blind and partially deaf.

4. The following are three tales of bizarre bird behavior. Which one is *not* true?

a. When a tornado trapped a red hen in a crate, she survived by eating her own eggs.

b. A mother duck alerted the police that her ducklings were trapped in a sewer by pulling on an officer's pant leg.

c. A heron rescued a goldfish that had jumped out of a pond.

5. Hold on—it's going to be one wild and crazy ride! Which one of the following amazing adventures is *not* true?

a. For six miles, two-year-old Allyson Hoary held onto the back of her dad's van, which was traveling at 60 miles per hour, until her dad saw her and pulled over.

b. Eight-year-old Deandra Anrig was carried 100 feet when her kite line got caught by a low-flying plane.

c. Five-year-old Freddie Lorenz sped downhill in a runaway grocery cart and across six lanes of street traffic until he finally crash-landed in some soft bushes.

6. An eight-year-old girl was carried 200 feet by a hawk before it dropped her into a nearby pond. She survived without injury!

Believe It!   **Not!**

7. An airplane flew 275 miles and landed safely with 4,700 holes in its wings and fuselage. The holes were made by a flock of geese that had flown head-on into the plane.

Believe It!   **Not!**

8. Frank Tower earned his place in the Ripley's files because he walked away from which unbelievable disasters?

a. Plane crashes in India, Japan, and China.

b. Three major shipwrecks, including the *Titanic*.

c. Three train wrecks, all within one year.

9. The lives of seven shipwrecked sailors were saved when their captain noticed that the seawater beneath their lifeboat changed color from blue to green as they drifted over a freshwater spring.

Believe It! **Not!**

10. Which of the following daring rescues never happened?

a. A surfer caught 17-month-old Sara Wolf when she fell overboard from a cruise ship.

b. A 12-year-old took the wheel of an out-of-control school bus, saving the lives of 33 kids on board.

c. A bus driver saved 30 passengers when he jammed his legs under the wheels to keep the bus from rolling over a cliff.

11. In 1991, a pod of dolphins performed which amazing rescue?

a. They saved eight passengers from a capsized yacht in California by carrying them to shore on their backs.

b. They protected a group of shipwrecked sailors from circling sharks in Florida.

c. They used their bodies to plug a large hole at the waterline of a sinking boat in New York's North River, saving hundreds of passengers.

12. Only one of the following daring doggy rescues is true. Can you pick out which one?

a. A Newfoundland dog swam to shore with a lifeline gripped in his teeth, ultimately saving 92 people from a wrecked ship that was breaking up in the stormy seas.

b. A golden retriever lay down in the middle of the road until a truck stopped. She then led the driver to her home where her owner was passed out on the floor.

c. A Chihuahua attacked a crocodile that had chomped down on the arm of her four-year-old owner.

13. Snail slime on the tracks can cause a train to derail.
Believe It!   Not!

14. Which of the following embarrassing situations is *not* true?

a. A man had to be rescued by firefighters when his tongue stuck to the inside of a freezer.

b. A man had to be rushed to the hospital after getting a curling iron stuck to his scalp.

c. A little girl had to be rescued by paramedics after she kissed her pet turtle and it wouldn't let go of her lip.

15. Which of the following shark stories is really true?

a. A surfer survived an attack by a great white shark by jamming his surfboard between the shark's jaws.

b. When a shark bit down on a swimmer's leg in northern Rhodesia, the swimmer clamped his teeth down on the tip of the shark's nose until it let go.

c. A scuba diver near Acapulco, Mexico, survived an attack by a ten-foot shark by swimming directly into the shark's mouth, past its jaws, and into its gullet.

Answer Key

Chapter 1

No Way!

Page 5:   **d.** moaning camel.

Page 7:   **a.** chasing it on horseback and lashing at it with a whip.

Page 8:   **c.** sporting a bad haircut.

Page 11:   **d.** supply all of Arizona with electricity.

Page 13   **b.** red spider spinning its web.

Page 15:   **b.** cover all of Manhattan to a depth of 28 stories.

Page 16:   **c.** horses refused to eat.

Page 19:   **d.** one million.

Page 20:   **b.** Galveston, Texas.

Brain Buster: **c.** is false.

Bonus Question: b.

Chapter 2

No Way!

Page 23:   **b.** carried it down a ladder.

Page 25:   **c.** from a seven-story apartment building.

Page 27:   **a.** lunged for a football and landed on a pencil that pierced his heart.

Page 29:   **c.** a freight train passed over her body.

Page 31:   **b.** using his drum as a life raft.

Page 32:   **c.** accidentally going over Niagara Falls.

Brain Buster: **d.** is false.

Bonus Question: b.

Chapter 3

No Way!

Page 35:   **a.** boat.

Page 36:   **d.** he mistook the *Titanic*'s emergency flares for fireworks.

Page 39:   **c.** a salmon (that was dropped by an eagle crashing through the windshield.

Page 41:   **b.** windmill.

Page 43:   **b.** everyone had been rescued.

Page 44:   **c.** whistling.

Brain Buster: a. is false.

Bonus Question: a.

Chapter 4

No Way!

Page 47:   **c.** canary.

Page 49:   **c.** the dams built by 60 beaver colonies.

Page 51:   **b.** an albatross.

Page 53:   **b.** kites.

Page 55:   **a.** the short circuit set off the doorbell, jarring him awake.

Page 56:   **c.** tying off a bleeding artery with dental floss.

Brain Buster: b. is false.

Bonus Question: c.

Chapter 5

No Way!

Page 59: **b.** coughed up the bullet.

Page 61: **a.** brain.

Page 63: **a.** her petticoat opened like a parachute.

Page 65: **a.** hanged for murder.

Page 67: **b.** was revived when pallbearers accidentally dropped his coffin on the road.

Page 69: **d.** pushing blocks of ice around.

Page 70: **a.** Theodore Roosevelt.

Page 72: **b.** fruit brought to him by a monkey.

Brain Buster: **c.** is false.

Bonus Question: a.

Pop Quiz

1. **Believe It!**
2. **a.**
3. **b.**
4. **c.**
5. **c.**
6. **Not!**
7. **Not!**
8. **b.**
9. **Believe It!**
10. **a.**
11. **b.**
12. **a.**
13. **Believe It!**
14. **b.**
15. **a.**

What's Your Ripley's Rank?

Ripley's Scorecard

Congrats! You've busted your brain over some of the oddest human behavior in the world and proven your ability to tell fact from fiction. Now it's time to rate your Ripley's knowledge. Are you an amazing survivor or an extreme escapist? Check out the answers in the answer key, and use this page to keep track of how many trivia questions you've answered correctly. Then add 'em up and find out how you rate.

Here's the scoring breakdown—give yourself:
★ **10 points** for every **No Way!** you answered correctly;

★ **20 points** for every fiction you spotted in the **Ripley's Brain Busters**;

★ **10** for every **Bonus Question** you answered right;

★ and **5** for every **Pop Quiz** question you answered correctly.

Here's a tally sheet:
Number of **No Way!** questions answered correctly: _____ x 5 = _____

Number of **Ripley's Brain Buster** questions answered correctly: _____ x 10 = _____

Number of **Bonus Questions** answered correctly: _____ x 5 = _____

Chapter Total: _____

Write your totals for each chapter and the Pop Quiz section in the spaces below. Then add them up to get your FINAL SCORE. Your FINAL SCORE decides how you rate:

Chapter 1 Total: _____

Chapter 2 Total: _____

Chapter 3 Total   _____

Chapter 4 Total: _____

Chapter 5 Total: _____

Pop Quiz Total: _____

FINAL SCORE: _____

525–301
Amazing Survivor!

You don't need to check with friends or look online to know you're right. You can tell the difference between fact and fiction on your own—no matter how bizarre the choices. You make it past the Bonus Round every time and you come out on top. You are the big winner, a breakout star, and a true survivor. You know a thing or two about surviving some tough challenges and you can't be fooled. If they passed out trophies for fiction detection, you'd win the lifetime achievement award. You ARE amazing. *Believe It!*

300–201
Escape Artist

You don't fall for tricks or teasers. You know what's up—the truth is the truth and you have an amazing ability to spot it. Exaggerations can't fool you, gossip doesn't throw you, and rumors are just rumors in your world. You love a good escape-from-danger story—they're inspiring and you know it. But you also know when you are being duped. You escape the trip ups with style. And you're rising in the ranks. Keep it up!

200–101
Close Call

You've escaped the ranks of the truly out of touch—but just barely. Don't give up. Your internal fact-checker may need some fine-tuning, but that's not a problem! The world is full of amazingly true tales as well as tantalizing tall tales. So you'll always have opportunities to test your Ripley's radar. Now you've got experience. New challenges lie ahead. Can you deal?

100–0
Extreme Escapist

You are in serious need of a Ripley's rescue! You have a hard time figuring out if someone is speaking in earnest or just pulling your leg. People like to tease you by getting you to believe outrageous tales of escape and rescue. That's okay. Maybe it's just not your thing, maybe you're too trusting, or maybe you just don't care. Whatever the reason, just keep in mind that the truth really can be stranger than fiction—and the world is constantly proving it!

Photo Credits

Ripley Entertainment Inc. and the editors of this book wish to thank the following photographers, agents, and other individuals for permission to use and reprint the following photographs in this book. Any photographs included in this book that are not acknowledged below are property of the Ripley Archives. Great effort has been made to obtain permission from the owners of all materials included in this book. Any errors that may have been made are unintentional and will gladly be corrected in future printings if notice is sent to Ripley Entertainment Inc., 5728 Major Boulevard, Orlando, Florida 32819.

7 Malagash Cottage/Tom McCoag/ Reprinted with permission from The Halifax Herald Limited

8 Johnstown Flood/National Park Service

9 Asteroid/NASA Photo Gallery

10 Peekskill Meteorite/Allan Lang/R. A. Langheinrich Meteorites/Ilion, New York/www.nyrockman.com;

10 Lightning; 37 Skydiver; 53 Dolphins/ CORBIS

12 Mount Pelée/Copyright Unknown

14 Mauna Loa/U.S.G.S. Photo Library, Denver, Colorado

15 Mount Saint Helens/Austin Post, U.S.G.S./CVO/Glaciology Project

17 Anchorage Earthquake/NOAA: National Geophysical Data Center, Boulder, Colorado

18 Mississippi River; 27 Black Cat; 38 Amsterdam Canal; 64 Tower of London/ PhotoDisc

40 *Andrea Doria*/Associated Press

42 *Endurance*/Frank Hurley/1914–16 Imperial Trans-Antarctic Expedition/ Royal Geographical Society Picture Library

50 Jambo/James Morgan/© Durrell Wildlife Conservation Trust

55 Fawn; 59 Coral Snake/Copyright 2001, Ripley Entertainment and its licensors

61 Sperm Whale/© 2000 Jonathan Bird/Oceanic Research Group, Inc.

63 George Washington Carver/Iowa State University/Special Collections Department

Contents

The Ripley Experience

A real-life "Indiana Jones," Robert Ripley traveled all over the world, tracking down amazing facts, oddities, and curiosities. A collector of just about anything and everything, Robert Ripley was never more delighted than when he happened to come across something really bizarre on one of his excursions. He was especially pleased if he could take it home with him. Shrunken heads, bone necklaces and bowls, medieval torture devices—these were the kinds of keepsakes he liked best, and they all eventually found places of honor in his home.

In keeping with Robert Ripley's fascination with the bizarre, it's not surprising that he was partial to those Believe It or Not! cartoons that dealt with the unexplainable. Robert Ripley loved a good story. If it happened to be about something ghoulish—such as the dying sculptor who carved a statue of himself, then transferred his own eyebrows, eyelashes, nails, and teeth to it—he liked it even better.

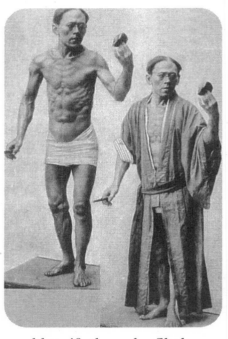

The Ripley archives are filled with tales of people suddenly waking up in morgues or sitting up in their coffins after they've been declared "dead." Whenever Robert Ripley heard stories like these, if he could verify them, he filed them away for use in future Believe It or Not! cartoons. Stories about ghosts and witches were also high up on the list of his favorite subjects.

Perhaps you've had an experience that was truly weird. Did you ever guess who was calling before you picked up the phone? Have you ever been overtaken by a feeling that felt stronger than a hunch? Can you tell when someone is staring at you before you turn around to look? If you answered "yes" to any of these questions, then you have a lot in common with the people featured in this book. Many of the ideas for Ripley's cartoons came from fans who wrote to tell him about spooky things that happened to them—about haunted houses they'd stayed in, spooky dreams that came true, or of their experiences with fortune-tellers and ESP.

You'll find all kinds of strange events in the pages of *Creepy Stuff.* You'll also get a chance to test your "stranger than fiction" smarts by answering the Believe It or Not! quizzes and Ripley Brain Buster in each chapter. Then you can take the special Pop Quiz at the end of the book and use the scorecard to find out your Ripley's Rank.

So get ready to enter a world of amazing people, places, and events—all of them unbelievable, but true.

Believe It!®

Most of us accept as truth only those things we can see, hear, touch, smell, or feel. Anything else must be science fiction. But if that's so . . .

Guesswork? In the early 1930s, Hubert Pearce guessed every card in the ESP test given by Dr. Joseph Rhine at Duke University. In fact, Pearce did just as well whether he was separated from the tester by only a screen or was in a separate building.

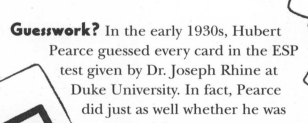

Believe It or Not!®

The ability to accurately predict what will happen in the future is called . . .

a. precognition.
b. X-ray vision.
c. good luck.
d. uncommon good sense.

Dead Right: In 1908, astrologer John Hazelrigg predicted that the men elected president of the United States in 1920, 1940, and 1960 would die during their terms of office—and they did.

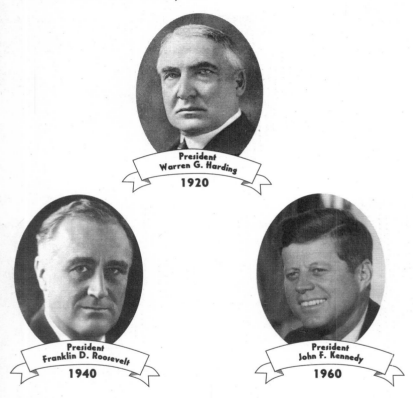

President
Warren G. Harding
1920

President
Franklin D. Roosevelt
1940

President
John F. Kennedy
1960

Bad Vibrations: In 1958, after a taxi driver was murdered in Chicago, psychic Peter Hurkos sat in the cab the driver had died in. As a result, Hurkos was able to describe the killer and provide the police with detailed information. The killer was caught.

Future Shock: In 1968, the famous astrologer Jeanne Dixon was about to give a speech at the Ambassador Hotel in Los Angeles. As she passed through the kitchen on her way to the room where she was scheduled to speak, Dixon stopped suddenly and blurted, "This is the place where Robert Kennedy will be shot. I can see him being carried out with blood on his face." Her prediction came true on June 6, 1968.

Common Senses: Hubert Pearce, John Hazelrigg, Peter Hurkos, and Jeanne Dixon all received information in an out-of-the-ordinary way. In each case, a sense other than the usual five senses was involved. Some people refer to this extra sense as the "sixth sense," or ESP.

Believe It or Not!®

The letters in the acronym ESP stand for the words . . .

a. extremely strange practices.
b. Earth, stars, and planets.
c. exact scientific predictions.
d. extrasensory perception.

Novel Predictions: In his 1898 novel, *Futility,* Morgan Robertson unknowingly predicted the sinking of the *Titanic* 14 years before it was built. In his story, an 800-foot ocean liner struck an iceberg on its maiden voyage one April night and sank. Even the size and capacity of the *Titanic* (3,000 passengers) matched Robertson's fictional ship, which was named the *Titan.*

Life Imitates Art: *Barzai,* a book written by German novelist F.H. Gratoff in 1908, described a Japanese-American war in which unprepared American troops led by a fictional General MacArthur lost battles at first, but then rallied to defeat the Japanese. Gratoff's book was an eerie foreshadowing of actual events featuring the real General MacArthur, who led American troops to victory during World War II.

Forger's Apprentice: The famous poet William Blake quit his job the first day that he was apprenticed to William Rylands, England's foremost engraver. Blake, who was 14 at the time, quit because when he looked at his employer, he had a chilling vision of him hanging dead on a gallows. Twelve years later, the vision came true when Rylands was hanged for forgery.

Believe It or Not!®

On the day I was born, my grandfather rode his horse around, shouting, "A United States senator has been born today!" He was right. Who was I?

a. Andrew Jackson
b. Harry S Truman
c. Lyndon B. Johnson
d. John F. Kennedy

Crystal Clear: One morning, four-year-old Crystal Guthrie, sobbing, told her mother that she had just seen her little dog killed by a truck. Anxiously, Crystal's mother went out to the backyard where she saw the puppy happily waiting for his breakfast. Minutes later, brakes screeched and a little dog cried out. Crystal's vision had come true.

Deep Reflection: In 1892, whaling captain Georges Vesperin consulted a fortune-teller in Paris, France, in a last-ditch effort to find his daughter, who had been missing for ten years. The fortune-teller said that all would be revealed in her "magic mirror." As soon as he saw the fortune-teller's mirror, Vesperin recognized it as the same one he had given to his daughter years before. Vesperin traced the mirror to a diver who had found it in the Indian Ocean while searching among the wreckage of a ship. Before long, Vesperin found his daughter living on the island of Amsterdam in the Indian Ocean.

Hot Tip: In the 1700s, well before the advent of instant media coverage, Swedish psychic Emanuel Swedenborg reported that a great fire had just broken out in Stockholm, 250 miles away. Two days later a letter reached him giving all the details of the fire—exactly as Swedenborg had described them.

Believe It or Not!®

As the most famous psychic of all time, I predicted World War II, the rise of Napoleon, the invention of the atomic bomb, and the French Revolution hundreds of years before they actually took place. My name is . . .

a. Merlin.
b. Rasputin.
c. Nostradamus.
d. Copernicus.

Picture Perfect: In 1963, psychic Irene Hughes was able to tell with uncanny accuracy what crimes each of 20 criminals had committed just by looking at their photographs.

Arresting Visions: Chris Robinson has been called "a force to be reckoned with" by Scotland Yard. Robinson is a janitor in Bedfordshire, England, by day and a psychic by night. His dream that five terrorists were planning atrocities in a hotel resulted in their arrest at that very hotel. After he had another dream that foretold an explosion at Bournemouth Pier, the police were able to locate the terrorists' bombs in time to save innocent lives.

ESP Law: Although psychic Robyn Slayden of Orlando, Florida, had no background in law, defense attorneys began calling on her in 1977 to help them select juries. Amazingly, Slayden could sense which jurors were prejudiced against defendants and predict the outcome of trials with stunning success.

Believe It or Not!®

Statistics show that more violent crimes are committed whenever . . .

a. there are high tides.
b. the moon is full.
c. it's hurricane season.
d. there's a total eclipse of the sun.

Dove Tale: In 1895, Maria Georghiu's son was kidnapped in Turkey. Seventeen years later, she dreamed that they were reunited on a journey to Cyprus. She booked passage at once. On the ship, she told a passenger about her son, describing a dove-shaped mole on his chest. The astonished man lifted his shirt to show Mrs. Georghiu the mole on his own chest. The man turned out to be her long-lost son!

Cat-astrophe: At 5:00 A.M. on November 2, 1951, Nova Churchill woke up crying, "I dreamed a black panther jumped on my mother and killed her." Later that day, Nova learned that her mother had had a heart attack while dusting a ceramic panther—at the exact moment Nova awoke.

In Plane Sight: "I could see this little girl screaming," spiritualist Francine Maness told the rescue team searching for a downed Piper Cub airplane in 1977. The searchers were then able to locate the twisted wreck in which only one member of the family had survived—a three-year-old girl.

Golden Touch: Psychic Anne Gehman can run her hands over a map and pick out places where oil will be found. She was recently shown ten potential sites and pointed to the four she was sure would be productive. Amazingly, all four turned out to be gushers.

Believe It or Not!®

Ten years ahead of time, Robert Burton (1577–1640), who wrote *The Anatomy of Melancholy*, accurately predicted the date of . . .

a. his first child's birth.
b. his own death from natural causes.
c. the onset of the bubonic plague.
d. the beginning of the Dark Ages.

Many animals can detect sounds and movements that cannot be perceived by humans . . .

Purr-fect Timing: Just before the 1925 Santa Barbara earthquake, a cat moved her newborn kittens from their home under a barn to higher ground. The quake destroyed a dam, flooding the barn.

Good Mews: Fluffy, a kitten owned by Mrs. Clyde McMillan, appeared at the office of a newspaper that had published a want ad asking for its return.

Sixth Scent: For many years, Harry Goodman's dog would walk alongside the railroad tracks with him. Then in 1968, a man was killed as he tried to cross the tracks. Afterward, the dog howled with fear whenever it approached the scene of the accident, even though it had not been present when the accident took place.

Written in the Stars: Ancient astronomers noticed the powerful effect that changes in the position of the sun and the moon had on Earth. If these heavenly bodies could influence the tides and the seasons, they reasoned, the stars and the planets could also have an effect on people.

The zodiac year is divided into 12 astrological signs, each named for a group of stars known as a constellation. According to astrologers, the sun enters a new sign each month.

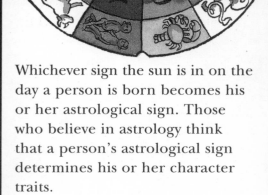

Believe It or Not!®

Many famous people have consulted astrologers, including United States President . . .

a. Dwight D. Eisenhower.
b. Richard M. Nixon.
c. Theodore Roosevelt.
d. Jimmy Carter.

Whichever sign the sun is in on the day a person is born becomes his or her astrological sign. Those who believe in astrology think that a person's astrological sign determines his or her character traits.

Taurus

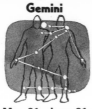

Apr. 20 – May 20

Gemini

May 21 – June 21

Cancer

June 22 – July 22

Aries

Mar. 21 – Apr. 19

Pisces

Feb. 19 – Mar. 20

Aquarius

Jan. 20 – Feb. 18

Star-tling Acquittal: Evangeline Adams was arrested in 1914 for being a fraud. In an effort to defend herself, she asked the judge to give her the date, time of day, and place of birth of someone known only to him. With this information, Adams drew up an astrological chart that described the person to a T. The judge was so impressed that he dismissed the case, and Adams was cleared of all charges. Whom had she described so well? None other than the judge's own son!

Astro-nomical Mistake: An astrologer warned Catherine de Médicis (1519–1589), queen of France, to "beware of St. Germain." Since her palace was in the St. Germain district of Paris, the Queen moved to another area at once. Not long afterward, she felt sick and had a priest called. That very evening she died unexpectedly. The name of the priest? Jullien de St. Germain.

Leo

July 23–Aug. 22

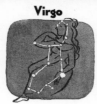

Virgo

Aug. 23–Sept. 22

Libra

Sept. 23–Oct. 23

Star Link: King George III and an ironworker named Samuel Hemming were both born in the same town at the

same moment on June 4, 1738. These astrological time-twins both married on September 8, 1761. Each had nine sons and six daughters. Both fell ill at exactly the same time and died on January 29, 1820. Was it a coincidence—or were their lives linked by the stars? What do you think?

Scorpio

Oct. 24–Nov. 21

Sagittarius

Nov. 22–Dec. 21

Capricorn

Dec. 22–Jan. 19

Believe It or Not!®

In what country do engaged couples usually have their horoscopes charted to set the wedding date and to find out whether their marriage is likely to succeed?

a. In Norway.
b. In Greece.
c. In India.
d. In Israel.

Star-crossed: One March night, Julius Caesar's wife dreamed that a statue of her husband was dripping with blood. The next morning, she warned him not to go to the senate, but he refused to listen. That day, March 15, Julius Caesar was stabbed to death by senators who feared he was becoming too powerful.

Serious Shell Shock: The ancient Greek playwright Aeschylus (525–426 B.C.) never went outdoors during storms because an astrologer had warned him that he would die by a blow from the heavens. One sunny day, Aeschylus was sitting outside when an eagle mistook his bald head for a rock. It dropped a huge tortoise on him to break its shell— and killed Aeschylus.

Believe It or Not!®

In New England, a prediction inserted into *The Old Farmer's Almanac* as a prank came true in July 1816 when . . .

a. it rained for 30 days.
b. it snowed three times.
c. there were three solar eclipses.
d. the temperature topped 100 degrees 14 days in a row.

Ripley's Believe It or Not! Brain Buster

The time has come to test your knowledge of the eerily bizarre, the inexplicably spooky, and the unbelievably strange!

The Ripley files are packed with info that's too out-there to believe. Each shocking oddity proves that truth is stranger than fiction. But it takes a keen eye, a sharp mind, and good instincts to spot the difference. Are you up for the challenge?

Each Ripley's Brain Buster contains groups of four unbelievable oddities. In each group of oddities only **one** is **false**. Read each extraordinary entry and circle whether you **Believe It!** or **Not!** And if you think you can handle it, take on the bonus question in each section. Then, flip to the end of the book where you'll find a place to keep track of your score and rate your skills.

Which is stranger, fact or fiction? Here is your first chilling challenge. Can you sense which one of the four strange tales below is 100% invented?

a. After pulling an "all-nighter" to study for a final exam in pre-calculus, 16-year-old Anika Storm dreamed that she was successfully solving math problems in her sleep. Anika was overjoyed during her exam the next day when she realized she had worked out most of the problems the night before—in her dreams!

Believe It!   **Not!**

113

b. In the 1930s, astrologer Evangeline Adams charted the horoscope of the United States. Since it was born on July 4, its sign is Cancer. According to its horoscope, it's a restless, inventive country with a great deal of talent.

Believe It!   Not!

c. Before an earthquake hit the French Riviera in 1887, horses all over the area refused to eat and tried to break out of their stalls.

Believe It!   Not!

d. Halley's comet can be seen from Earth only once every 75 years. When Samuel Langhorne Clemens, also known as Mark Twain, was born in 1835, the comet could be seen in the sky. Twain predicted that just as he had come in with the comet, he would go out with it. In April 1910, the comet returned, and on April 21, 1910, Mark Twain passed away.

Believe It!   Not!

BONUS QUESTION

John Dee invented the crystal ball in the mid-1500s. What was his occupation?

a. He was a fortune-teller in Granada, Spain.

b. He was a renowned glass blower and shopkeeper in Paris, France.

c. He was a mathematician and president of Manchester College in England.

When two or more remarkable things happen at the same time, most of us chalk it up to coincidence. But some stories are so amazing it's hard to believe fate might not also be at work.

Same Time, Next Year:

Brothers Neville and Erskine L. Ebbin of Bermuda died one year apart after being struck by the same taxi that was being driven by the same driver and carrying the same passenger.

Believe It or Not!®

In the heat of battle, Patrick Ferguson had the chance to shoot a man in the back, but his sense of honor would not allow him to. The name of the man Ferguson spared was . . .

a. Theodore Roosevelt.
b. Thomas Jefferson.
c. Dwight D. Eisenhower.
d. George Washington.

Coat of Doom: Jabez Spicer of Leyden, Massachusetts, was killed by two bullets on January 25, 1787, in Shays' Rebellion at Springfield Arsenal. Jabez was wearing the coat his brother Daniel had been wearing when he was killed by two bullets on March 5, 1784. The bullets that killed Jabez passed through the same two holes that had been made when Daniel was killed three years earlier.

Pocket Protector:

Detective Melvin Lobbet of Buffalo, New York, was shot by a .38 caliber revolver at close range. He was saved when the bullet hit his badge—which he had dropped into his coat pocket only a moment before.

Believe It or Not!®

Angel Santana of New York City escaped unharmed when a robber's bullet bounced off his . . .

a. pants zipper.
b. shatterproof sunglasses.
c. wedding band.
d. right biceps.

Shattering Talent: In the 1800s, Etienne Laine, a vegetable peddler who lived in Paris, France, came to the attention of the director of the Royal Academy of Music when his shouts of "Buy my asparagus" shattered a window in the director's office. The director was so impressed he made Laine a star tenor in the Paris opera.

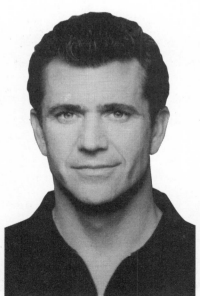

Mugging for the Camera: Mel Gibson was mugged the night before his first screen test. It's a good thing he decided to go anyway because when he got there, he found out that the role called for someone who looked weary, beaten up, and scared. He got the part— the starring role in *Mad Max*.

Mc-Multiples: George McDaniels and his entire family—father, mother, sister, two brothers, and an uncle—were all born on the same day of the year.

Statistical Leap:

Elizabeth Elchlinger of Parma, Ohio, and her son Michael were both born on February 29, which comes only once every four years. The odds of a mother and son being born on that date are over two million to one.

Rekindled Kin: Different families adopted identical twins Mark Newman and Jerry Levey five days after they were born. Both twins grew up to be firefighters, and in 1954, they found each other entirely by chance at a firefighters' convention.

Parallel Lives: The "Jim" twins were separated at birth and raised apart. Yet a 1979 study revealed that both brothers married women named Linda, then divorced and married women named Betty. One brother named his first son James Alan and the other named his James Allen. Both brothers named their dog Toy and drove the same make of car. Both did well in math, liked woodworking, and suffered from frequent headaches.

Branded at Birth: In 1901, the Meudelle twins were born in Paris, France. Each child had a birthmark on one shoulder that formed the initials of the maternal grandparent after whom the twin was named. The boy bore the letters T R and was named for his grandfather, Theodore Rodolphe. His sister bore the letters B V and was named for her grand-mother, Berthe Violette.

Believe It or Not!®

The astrological sign for June is twins. This sign is called . . .

a. Gemini.
b. Sagittarius.
c. Taurus.
d. Libra.

Ate His Fish and His Words: Moses Carlton, a wealthy shipping magnate from Wiscasset, Maine, threw his gold ring into the Sheepscot River and boasted, "There is as much chance of my dying a poor man as there is of ever finding that ring again." A few days later, Carlton found the ring in a fish served to him in a restaurant. Soon after, President Madison placed an embargo on American ships, causing Carlton to lose his fortune, and sure enough, he died a poor man.

Died Laughing: Although apparently in good health, English dramatist Edward Moore sent his own obituary to the newspapers as a joke, giving the next day as his date of death. Moore suddenly became ill and died—the next day!

Disarmed: The sixth Viscount of Strathallan on the Isle of Mulligan, Scotland, swore he would give his good right arm to win a lawsuit. He won the case. A month later, he was inspecting a factory when a flywheel cut off his right arm below the elbow.

Unlucky Streaks:

Lightning struck the house of R. Scott Andres of Virgin Arm, Newfoundland, Canada, on July 4, 1985. The very next night, his sister's house in North Bay, Ontario, was also struck by lightning.

Believe It or Not!®

When his soldiers complained about being stationed overseas, an army captain responded by saying, "I'd rather be here than be president of the United States." The name of this future president was . . .

a. John F. Kennedy.
b. Harry S Truman.
c. Dwight D. Eisenhower.
d. Andrew Jackson.

Venetian Bind: Francesco delle Barche, who lived in Venice during the 14th century, invented a catapult that could hurl a 3,000-pound missile. Unfortunately, he became entangled in it during a battle and was hurtled into the center of the town. His body struck his own wife, and both were killed instantly.

Deeply Troubling: In 1988, Wright Skinner, Jr., fell into Winyah Bay in Georgetown, South Carolina, on February 13, becoming the fifth person lost in its murky depths on the same date within 11 years.

Common Scents: A traveler standing in a railway station in Stillwater, Oklahoma, was eating an apple when a stranger approached and said, "That smells like a North Carolina apple." The traveler replied, "It is. I'm from North Carolina." "So am I," said the stranger. It turned out that the two men were brothers who had not met in 30 years.

Believe It or Not!®

Triskaidekaphobia is so widespread that 90 percent of the high-rise buildings in the United States have no . . .

a. 13th floor.
b. mirrors in the lobbies.
c. pictures of black cats.
d. cracks on the floors.

Scat, Cat—or Not? If a black cat ran across your path in the United States, you might expect to be in for some bad luck. In England, on the other hand, a black cat crossing your path means you can expect good fortune, and a white cat signifies bad luck.

Two of America's most beloved presidents are linked by an eerie set of coincidences . . .

✦ Both John F. Kennedy and Abraham Lincoln were deeply involved in the civil rights issue of his era. In Lincoln's time, the issue was slavery; in Kennedy's time, it was segregation.

✦ Both were assassinated.

✦ Lincoln's assassin, John Wilkes Booth, was born in 1839. Kennedy's assassin, Lee Harvey Oswald, was born in 1939.

✦ Lincoln had a secretary named Kennedy who warned him not to go to the theater the night he died. Kennedy had a secretary named Lincoln who warned him not to go to Dallas.

- ✦ Both were shot on a Friday.

- ✦ Each wife was present when her husband was shot.

- ✦ Booth shot Lincoln in a theater and ran into a warehouse. Oswald shot Kennedy from a warehouse and ran into a theater.

- ✦ Both were succeeded by men named Johnson.

- ✦ Both Johnsons were Democrats from the South.

- ✦ The Johnson who succeeded Lincoln was born in 1808. The Johnson who succeeded Kennedy was born in 1908.

- ✦ Both presidents' last names have seven letters; their successors' first and last names combined have 13 letters; and their assassins' first and last names combined have 15 letters.

Believe It or Not!®

In 1872, Baron Roemire de Tarazone of France was murdered by an assassin named Claude Volbonne. Twenty-one years later, his son was murdered . . .

a. on the very same street.
b. by the son of Claude Volbonne.
c. by another Claude Volbonne who was unrelated to his father's murderer.
d. on the exact same date.

Holy Smoke Screen:

The 14th Dalai Lama of Tibet was held prisoner of the Communist Chinese in his own palace. He planned his escape on the afternoon of March 17, 1959. Although Chinese troops surrounded the palace and huge searchlights were trained on the building, the Dalai Lama and 80 companions escaped under cover of a sudden sandstorm.

Hugh Who? In 1664, 1785, and 1820, three unrelated men, all named Hugh Williams, were the sole survivors of three different disasters at sea.

Believe It or Not!®

The laws of chance are not enough to explain the large number of ships and aircraft that have disappeared in an area of the Atlantic Ocean called the . . .

a. Bahamas Quadrangle.
b. Bermuda Triangle.
c. Granada Square.
d. Colombia Circle.

Below are four creepy coincidences that will challenge your ability to tell fact from fiction. Only one of these eerie tales is false. Can you tell which one? Take a chance!

a. In Howe, Indiana, the "Animal Woman" lived with skunks and did not bathe or change her clothes for 25 years. When she was finally given a bath, she died ten days later!

Believe It!   **Not!**

b. In 1965, Anna Moses of Pittsburgh, Pennsylvania, comforted an older woman who was crying in a neighborhood park. She bought the woman a cup of tea, and sat with her until she had calmed down. Thirty years later, Anna received a letter from a lawyer alerting her that the older woman—who had inherited a large fortune after the death of a beloved aunt—had recently passed away and left Anna $500,000 in gratitude for her kindness.

Believe It!   **Not!**

c. Stephen Law of Markham, Ontario, was searching for a ring that his father had lost in five feet of lake water. He didn't find his father's ring, but he stumbled upon a topaz ring his grandmother had lost 41 years earlier in the same lake!

Believe It!   **Not!**

127

d. A bank customer who tried to cash a check in Monroe Township, New Jersey, was arrested when the teller turned out to be the Linda Brandimato to whom the check was made out.

Believe It!   Not!

• •

BONUS QUESTION

Some might say the marriage of Mr. and Mrs. Joseph Meyerberg of Brooklyn, New York, was "meant to be." What did they discover after their wedding?

a. That their great-grandparents came from the same small town in Germany and were childhood sweethearts.

b. That her Social Security number was 064-01-8089, and his Social Security number was 064-01-8090.

c. That they both attended kindergarten at the same school in Germany and were best friends before their families immigrated to Brooklyn.

Most of us would scoff at the idea that unknown forces could possess an inanimate object, but then again . . .

Hope Against Hope: Bad luck has followed the Hope Diamond ever since a jeweler brought it from India to France in the 17th century. The jeweler was killed by a pack of mad dogs. In 1793, owners Louis XVI and Marie Antoinette were beheaded. After American socialite Evalyn Walsh McLean bought the diamond in 1911, her son was killed in a car accident, her daughter died of an overdose, and her husband died in a mental hospital. Today, the blue 45.52-carat Hope Diamond is in the Smithsonian, which, so far at least, remains intact.

Believe It or Not!®

An arch is all that's left of an ancient Roman bridge over the Ludias River in Greece. The rest of the stones were looted by local farmers, who only stopped when they realized that everyone who had carried away stones . . .

a. died within a year.
b. lost all their teeth.
c. lost their farms.
d. became lepers.

Star Ship: In 1647, an English ship loaded with colonists disappeared. A year later, witnesses saw the ship appear in the sky over New England with astounding clarity. Henry Wadsworth Longfellow's poem, "The Phantom Ship," commemorates this event.

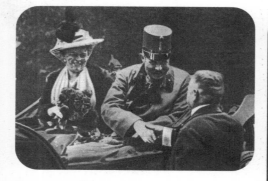

Possessed! The assassination of Archduke Franz Ferdinand of Austria started World War I. The car he was assassinated in is now in a Vienna museum. But before it was taken off the road, it was in *nine* accidents.

Believe It or Not!®

One night, the four Harner sisters, who slept in four separate bedrooms, were instantly killed by the same . . .

a. meteorite.
b. .38 caliber bullet.
c. firecracker.
d. bolt of lightning.

Trunk-ated Engagement:

The schooner *Susan and Eliza* was wrecked in a storm off Cape Ann, Massachusetts. Aboard was one of the shipowner's daughters, Susan Hichborn, who was on her way to her wedding in Boston. All 33 passengers perished. The only trace of the ship ever found was a trunk bearing Hichborn's initials and containing her possessions. It was cast ashore at the feet of her waiting fiancé.

That Sinking Feeling:

A Mississippi riverboat called the *Jo Daviess* sank after only three trips. Its engines were removed and installed on the steamboat *Reindeer,* and it sank, too. Salvaged once again, the engines were installed on the *Reindeer II,* which sank almost immediately. The engines were then used on the *Colonel Clay,* which sank after two trips. Next, the engines were installed on the S.S. *Monroe.* It was destroyed by fire. Salvaged for the fifth time, the engines were used in a gristmill, which burned to the ground.

Car Trouble: On his way to Salinas, California, movie star James Dean was driving 80 miles per hour when he was killed in a head-on collision. Investigators were puzzled by evidence that suggested that Dean, who was an expert driver, had done nothing to avoid the crash. Fans who flocked to the grisly scene were injured as they tried to remove pieces of the wreckage.

A garage mechanic, hired to restore the sports car, broke both legs when it fell on him. Two doctors bought parts from the car to reuse in their own race cars. After the parts were installed, one doctor died and the other suffered serious injury. The two undamaged tires were sold to a man who had to be hospitalized after they both blew out at the same time.

The California Highway Patrol planned to use the remains of the car in an auto show, but the night before the show opened, a fire broke out, destroying every vehicle but Dean's car, which escaped unscathed. The car was once again bound for Salinas when the driver lost control of the truck that was carrying it.

The driver was killed instantly. Dean's car rolled off the truck. The next effort to display the car also ended in calamity when the car, which had been carefully welded back together, inexplicably broke into 11 pieces. The

Florida police arranged to take the car for a safety display. But after the pieces of the car were crated and loaded onto a truck, the car disappeared, never to be seen again.

Believe It or Not!®

Five motorcycle racers who were killed in crashes over a period of four years had at least one thing in common when they died. They all . . .

a. wore the same helmet.
b. drove the same motorcycle.
c. had the same license plate number.
d. were talking on their cell phones.

A Grave Curse: Because the ancient Egyptians believed that the spirits of the dead returned to their bodies, they mummified bodies and sealed them in tombs. To open a tomb was to offend the gods. Between 1900 and 1976, more than 30 people who studied Egyptian tombs came to an untimely end. Could their deaths be the result of an ancient curse on the life of whoever dared enter?

Tut Tut! Tutankhamen—Tut for short—was pharaoh, or king, of Egypt from 1361 to 1352 B.C. He is one of the best known pharaohs because his tomb and its contents remained intact for more than 3,000 years. Though robbers stripped most pharaohs' tombs, Tut's wasn't discovered until 1922. Inside were thousands of treasures, including a jewel-encrusted throne made of silver and gold, and three ornamented nested coffins. Tut's body lay in the innermost coffin, which was made of solid gold.

Tomb and Doom: Famous Egyptologist Professor James Breasted, who was present at the first opening of Tut's tomb, died of fever. Shortly after loading the plane with artifacts from Tut's tomb, crew members suffered injuries.

Believe It or Not!®

In the 16th century, some European medicines were made of rhubarb mixed with ground-up . . .

a. mummy coffins.
b. hair from mummified cats.
c. mummy wrappings.
d. mummies.

Mummy Ship: The ocean liner *Titanic* was thought to be unsinkable. Could its sad fate have had something to do with its cargo, which included 2,200 passengers, 40 tons of potatoes, 12,000 bottles of mineral water, 7,000 sacks of coffee, 35,000 eggs—and an Egyptian mummy? There's really no way to tell.

Grave Warning: The tomb of the Turkish conqueror Tamerlane (1336–1405) in Samarkand, East Uzbekistan, bore an inscription that read, "If I should be brought back to Earth, the greatest of all wars will engulf this land." Soviet scientists, interested in studying historical burial practices, opened the tomb on June 22, 1941, at 5:00 A.M. and removed Tamerlane's mummified body. At the same moment, World War II broke out in Samarkand.

Homing Instinct: The *Dora*, originally a whaler from Port Townsend, Washington, was converted into a steamer by the Alaska Steamship Lines. In 1907, she lost her anchor in Cold Bay, Alaska, drifted without a compass for 92 days, and ended up at her old homeport in Washington. When the ship was taken out of the water, it was found that her hull had been badly damaged, and that the ship had been kept afloat by a rock wedged in the gaping hole.

Hands Off: In 1884, Walter Ingram returned to England, with the mummified hand of an ancient Egyptian princess. Clutched in the hand was a gold plaque that read, "Whoever takes me to a foreign land will die a violent death and his bones will never be found!" Four years later, Ingram was trampled to death by an elephant in Somaliland. He was buried in a dry riverbed, but when an expedition was sent to bring Ingram's body back to England, they discovered that it had been washed away by a flood.

Believe It or Not!®

A Gloucester schooner, wrecked and abandoned by its crew, blew a shrieking blast on its foghorn before plunging to the bottom of the sea. Its story inspired Henry Wadsworth Longfellow to write the poem, "The Wreck of the . . .

a. Maine."
b. Hesperus."
c. Bounty."
d. Pequod."

Queen-in-the-Box:

The night before Queen Elizabeth I of England was to be buried, her casket mysteriously exploded. Though the coffin was destroyed, the queen's body was unharmed.

Not So Safe:

Blasi Hoffman, a rich miser of Borken, Germany, locked his money in a safe in his room every night and slept with the key under his pillow. The moment he died on the night of July 9, 1843, the safe door flew open.

Remote Control: In

World War I, a British observation plane on the western front flew in wide circles for several hours and then landed without mishap—even though its pilot and observer were both dead.

Believe It or Not!®

Thirty years after killing a man on the island of Malta, sculptor Melchiore Caffa (1631–1687) felt so guilty that he created a statue of his victim to mark the grave. While putting the final touches on the sculpture . . .

a. the ghost of Caffa's victim appeared.
b. it toppled over, crushing Caffa to death.
c. it disintegrated.
d. Caffa was murdered.

You are entering a world of facts too bizarre to believe. You'll Believe It!—or Not! Three of the Ripley's oddities below are totally true. One is fully fictitious. Can you spot the fiction?

a. Many people in the mountain towns of Nepal believe that wearing mismatched socks while attempting a difficult climb up a mountain is bad luck. It is considered disrespectful—an affront to the mountain and to the gods.

Believe It!   **Not!**

b. In 1991, an appeals court in New York State officially declared a house in Nyack, New York, to be haunted.

Believe It!   **Not!**

c. Many hotels in China don't label the fourth floor because the character for four in the Chinese written language is the same as the character for death.

Believe It!   **Not!**

d. A poplar, planted in Jena, Germany, in 1815, to celebrate the end of the Napoleonic War with France, toppled suddenly 99 years later on August 1, 1914, the start of World War I.

Believe It!   **Not!**

BONUS QUESTION

The eye of the ancient Egyptian god Horus was a symbol of protection and healing. What contemporary symbol is derived from it?

a. The sign Rx used by physicians on prescriptions.

b. The @ symbol used in e-mail addresses.

c. The peace symbol.

Nearly a dozen ghosts have haunted the White House, many of them former presidents. Among those who have admitted to seeing these ghosts are Mary Todd Lincoln, Harry Truman, and William Howard Taft.

Ghostly Image: Of course there's no such thing as a ghost . . . but then who is that standing behind Mary Todd Lincoln in this photo taken many years after Abraham Lincoln's death? Is it Lincoln's ghost? An optical illusion? A fake?

Believe It or Not!®

Even though no one is there, family members often hear children running and laughing on the third floor of the Custis-Lee Mansion, which was once lived in by . . .

a. Bruce Lee.
b. Light-Horse Harry Lee.
c. Gypsy Rose Lee.
d. Robert E. Lee.

Haunted Hallways: Before he died, Abraham Lincoln told several people of a dream he'd had. In the dream, Lincoln saw a coffin lying in state in the East Room. When he asked who had died, he was told, "The president. He's been assassinated." Not long afterward, President Lincoln was murdered by an assassin's bullet. Since then, many people who have worked in the White House have reported seeing Lincoln's ghost roaming the hallways.

Jolly Spirit: When Andrew Jackson was president, his bedroom was in what is now called the Rose Room. After President Jackson died, deep laughter was heard coming from his room. Those who worked in the White House during his term of office recognized Jackson's laugh. The laugh has been heard at least once every four years ever since.

Ghostly Hijinks:

The students at Burnley School of Professional Art in Seattle, Washington, have grown accustomed to seeing some unusual sights—desks that appear to be moving

under their own steam, locked doors that open mysteriously by themselves, the sound of footsteps on vacant staircases. Who could be responsible? Could it be the ghosts of students past?

Believe It or Not!®

What English landmark is said to be haunted by the ghosts of Sir Walter Raleigh and Anne Boleyn?

a. Buckingham Palace
b. Westminster Abbey
c. Windsor Castle
d. The Tower of London

Spirited Uproars:

She was beheaded by her husband, King Henry VIII, so why do the servants at Hampton Court in England swear that Catherine Howard still roams the castle? It must be the bloodcurdling screams that come from her old rooms.

Friendly Phantom: It's a good thing that Christoph Gluck, a German composer who lived during the 1700s, believed in ghosts. Gluck got spooked after seeing an apparition of himself enter his bedroom and refused to sleep there that night. The next morning, Gluck discovered that the bedroom ceiling had collapsed over his bed and would have killed him had he slept there.

Sleepless in Zurich: For 900 years, no one has been able to stay overnight at a Hapsburg castle near Zurich, Switzerland. Why? Because the ghost of a murdered woman still screams in terror each and every night without fail. As recently as 1978, one unbeliever, Horst Von Roth, who tried to stay the night, fled the haunted dwelling in horror.

Beatlemania? The members of the world-famous rock group the Beatles felt that they were able to speak to and receive messages from their manager, Brian Epstein—even after he had died.

Angelic Apparitions: When the Wilcoxes' car broke down in New Mexico in 1966, a Mexican family whose surname was Angel offered them food and shelter. A year later, Mr. Wilcox stopped by to say hello, but to his

surprise, a different family was living in the house, and no one had ever heard of the Angel family.

The Ghost at the Top of the Stairs:

During the 1970s, actor Richard Harris was constantly awakened at 2:00 A.M. by the banging of closet doors and the sound of little feet running up and down the tower stairs of his home. Only after he built a nursery at the top of the stairs and filled it with toys did the ghost become better behaved. The actor says he knew the ghost was a child because old records revealed that an eight-year-old boy was buried in the tower.

Believe It or Not!®

In the 1750s, Nellie Macquillie was drowned in a pool in North Carolina. Her ghost is still seen nearby, carrying her head under her arm. She's known as . . .

a. Headless Nellie.
b. No Noggin Nellie.
c. the Pool Ghoul.
d. the Headless Mermaid.

Riches from Witches: Johannesburg Castle in Aschaffenburg, Germany, was constructed between 1607 and 1614. It was paid for entirely with funds confiscated from women who were convicted of witchcraft.

Eyewitness: The Witch's Eye, near Thann, France, was used for years as a prison for persons accused of witchcraft. It is the only part of Englesbourg Castle that is still standing.

Believe It or Not!®

If you live in Phoenix, Arizona, and your ancestors were witches, you might want to join an organization called . . .

a. Wicked Men of the West.
b. Broom Brood.
c. Sorcerer's Apprentices.
d. Sons of Witches.

Witch Hysteria: In 1692, several young girls claimed they were being tormented by witches. As a result, 19 people in Salem, Massachusetts, were arrested, convicted of witchcraft, and hanged. One man, who refused to stand trial, was crushed to death.

Witch, Be Gone: Glass balls manufactured in the United States in the 19th century were hung in the windows of homes to ward off the evil spells of witches.

Probing Examinations: Sixteenth-century European witch-hunters used sharp probes to search victims for "the devil's mark"—skin areas such as a healed scar that did not bleed.

Burning Crusade:

Mathew Hopkins was the "witch-finder general" in 17th-century England, traveling around the country on his horrible missions. He determined guilt by throwing a suspected witch into a well. If the person floated, he or she was a witch and had to be burned at the stake.

Believe It or Not!®

In 1474, in the city of Basel, Switzerland, an animal was tried and found guilty of witchcraft. Was it a . . .

a. rooster for laying an egg?
b. hen for crowing cock-a-doodle-doo?
c. dog for not barking at intruders?
d. cow for not giving milk?

Brain Buster

You know the drill. Go for it!

a. In 1574, Margaret Erskine of Dryburgh, Scotland, died suddenly and was buried in the family mausoleum. That night, when the sexton (the person who takes care of church property) tried to steal a ring from her finger, the dead woman sat up in her coffin and screamed. She lived for another 51 years!

Believe It!   **Not!**

b. Peter III of Russia was murdered in 1762 when he was 34 years old. He was crowned Emperor of Russia 34 years after his death—his coffin had to be opened so the crown could be placed on his head!

Believe It!   **Not!**

c. In 1985, Eric Villet of Orléans, France, was declared officially dead after doctors failed to revive him with heart massage and oxygen. He started breathing on his own three days later while lying in the morgue!

Believe It!   **Not!**

d. On May 16, 1997, William A. Hershorn was cutting through the cemetery on his way home. He tripped over a newly placed tombstone with the name W.A. Hershorn engraved on it along with the date of death, 5/16/97. Panicked, William ran out of the cemetery and into the street—where he was struck and killed by a car.

Believe It!   **Not!**

BONUS QUESTION

The White River Monster Sanctuary in Newport, Arkansas, was created by the state legislature for what purpose?

a. To make it illegal to vandalize a statue of a sea monster believed to have healing powers.

b. To make it illegal to "molest, kill, or trample" a legendary sea monster.

c. To make it illegal to kill or harm a Gila monster, a large black-and-orange venomous lizard that populates the area.

Just Plain Weird

Some real-life stories are wilder than the tallest tales dreamed up by the most imaginative writers of fiction.

Queen of Denial: After the death of her husband, Prince Albert, in 1861, England's Queen Victoria continued to have his formal evening clothes laid out every day at Windsor Castle for the next 40 years.

Believe It or Not!®

On display at the Museum of the History of Science in Florence, Italy, is Galileo's . . .

a. first telescope.
b. middle finger.
c. notebook.
d. skull.

Cool Reception: Imelda Marcos threw a party in honor of her late husband's 73rd birthday. The former president of the Philippines attended, but was not very good company since he arrived frozen in his casket.

Head Trip: The secret of head-shrinking had always been fiercely guarded until Robert Ripley somehow got hold of it. This is what he found out about the process. First, the victim's head was removed. Then the scalp was slit down the middle, and the skull was pulled through the opening. Next, the lips were sewn up and hot stones and sand were poured into the cavity. Finally, the head was sewn shut and boiled in herbs until it had shrunk to the

size of a fist. The Jivaros of the Amazon forest in South America believed that to possess a warrior's head was to keep for oneself all the powers of the original owner.

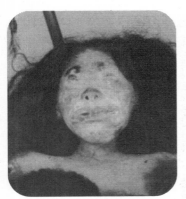

Ghoulish Figure: The Jivaros did not typically shrink female heads. However, the upper bodies of women were often prepared in the early 19th century to sell to tourists.

Saved by a Whisker: While on a ship at sea, the three-year-old Marquise de Maintenon was pronounced dead and sewn up in a sack to be thrown overboard. Luckily, her pet kitten had crawled inside the sack and began meowing during the funeral service. The mourners stopped the service, opened the sack, and discovered that the little girl was breathing. She later became the second wife of Louis XIV, and lived to the age of 84.

Babe in the Woods: Diego Quiroga, who was separated from his wife while fleeing Madrid during the French Invasion of 1811, found a newborn infant crying in a snow-covered field. He wrapped the baby in a blanket and carried her to the village of Venta de Pinar. There he learned the infant was his own daughter, born only a few hours earlier and abandoned by a nursemaid in the confusion of the flight.

Believe It or Not!®

Joseph Friedrich (1790– 1873) of Berlin, Germany, made an ivory miniature of the Church of St. Nicholas. The model developed a crack, and a few weeks later, the church did, too—in the same exact spot. Friedrich . . .

a. was publicly hanged.
b. lost his mind.
c. died of fright.
d. was struck by lightning.

Windows of the Soul:

Bedrooms in Grisons, Switzerland, have a tiny window that is opened only when the occupant is dying, to permit his or her soul to escape.

Believe It or Not!®

Some people pay psychics to tell their future by studying . . .

a. the palm of their hand.
b. the sole of their foot.
c. their knees.
d. their eyes.

Mourning Pigeon:

A strange occurrence marked the burial service for Captain Joseph Belain, the man who had dedicated his life to saving the carrier pigeon from extinction. As if in tribute, a carrier pigeon flew in from the sea, perched on the bier, and stayed until the service was over.

Bumped Off: Countess Marie Arco of Austria found $50,000 in gold ducats in her garden, but never spent a single coin. Instead, she put the money in a chest and strapped it to the luggage rack inside her coach. She took the fortune everywhere she went until, on June 23, 1848, a bump in the road dislodged the treasure chest, which fell and killed her.

Three Times a Charm: In 1803, Joseph Samuels, sentenced to death by hanging for burglary in Hobart Town, Australia, was granted a reprieve by the governor after the rope broke three times.

Skullcap: In the Sainte Chapelle church in Paris, France, there is a bust of King Louis IX (1214–1270). What makes this sculpture so remarkable? A piece of the monarch's skull lies directly beneath the royal crown that sits on top of the sculpture's head.

Boning Up: Jeremy Bentham, who founded London's University Hospital in 1827, declared that no board meeting should ever take place without him. After his death in 1832, his cadaver was propped up at the conference table. Today, a wax replica sits in for Bentham, though his real head rests on the table. Of course, since Bentham cannot take an active part in the meetings, he is recorded as "present, but not voting."

Such a Headache: In 1867, William Thompson of Omaha, Nebraska, was shot by Native Americans of the Cheyenne tribe. Thinking he was dead, they removed his scalp. Imagine their surprise when Thompson regained consciousness, grabbed his scalp, and ran. He later donated the scalp to the Omaha Public Library.

"Bonified" Retreat: Six miles east of Prague in the Czech Republic, there is an 800-year-old chapel decorated entirely with bones. Bones are everywhere, giving the chapel a delicate, lacy appearance. A Czech woodcarver named Frantisek Rint bedecked the chapel with the bones of 40,000 people because, as the story goes, the nearby cemetery was filled, and many others were dying to be buried there.

Believe It or Not!®

One piece of cargo that traveled on the space shuttle *Discovery* in 1990 was a . . .

a. human skull.
b. monkey brain.
c. tadpole.
d. human eyeball.

Guilt Trip: In 1650, Oswald Kröl of Lindau, Germany, was convicted and executed for murder. Kröl was later vindicated. From that day on, his skeleton was propped up before the judge who had pronounced the death sentence.

Dead Ringer: Although he was well grounded in science, Thomas Edison was also interested in the psychic world. In fact, he invented (but never patented) a machine for communicating with the dead.

Believe It or Not!®

In Borneo, a human skull is placed between the bride and groom at weddings as a symbol . . .

a. of death, the penalty for infidelity.
b. that love can outlast death.
c. of ancestors watching over them.
d. that their children will outlive them.

Don't Leave Home Without It: Victorian vampire prevention kits had everything you'd need to survive a Transylvania vacation— a garlic necklace, a vial of holy water, a wooden stake, and a crucifix-shaped gun that fired silver bullets.

Tunnel Vision: The Tunnel of Posilipo in Naples, Italy, is 80 feet high, 22 feet wide, and $1/2$ mile long. It is completely illuminated by the sun only once each year— at sunset on Halloween.

Soulful Celebration: In Mexico, it is believed that the dead return once a year to visit with their loved ones. To make them feel welcome, relatives celebrate the Day of the Dead on the first two days in November, bedecking the graves with flowers and candles (*see color insert*).

Graveyard Bash: In Madagascar, an island off the coast of Africa, many people believe that honoring their dead loved ones with a sumptuous feast will bring the entire family good fortune. Every five years or so, families observe a holiday called Famadihana. The families remove their dead relatives from their tombs, tell them the most important family news, and even dance with them. Afterward, they give the bodies new shrouds and return them to their graves. (*See color insert.*)

Body of Work: In the 1700s, Honoré Fragonard, an anatomy teacher at a veterinary school, created bizarre objects out of animal and human cadavers. According

to Christophe Degueurce, curator of the Fragonard Museum, Fragonard obtained cadavers from veterinary schools, medical schools, executions, and even fresh graves. He stripped them of skin, dissected all the muscles and nerves, injected the blood vessels with wax, and steeped the bodies in alcohol for days. Finally, he stretched them into elaborate poses and dried them with hot air.

Ouch! When a woodcarver named Masakichi found out he was dying, he decided to leave a "living image" of himself to his beloved. After painstakingly plucking the hair from every pore in his body, he inserted each one in a corresponding position on a statue of himself he had carved. He included his eyebrows and eyelashes, then for the finishing touches, he pulled out his fingernails, toenails, and teeth, and attached them to his sculpture.

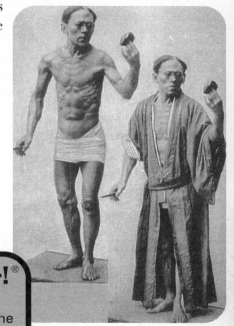

Believe It or Not!®

At Mount Minobu, Japan, Buddhists pay homage at the grave of Nichieren, founder of a Japanese sect, by . . .

a. allowing five candles on each outstretched arm to burn down to the flesh.
b. staying at the grave for two weeks without food or shelter.
c. walking on their knees to the gravesite.
d. holding their arms above their heads for an entire day.

Spin Cycle: The tombstone of Charles Merchant is a huge black granite sphere that has revolved on its stone pedestal once every year since it was built—despite the use of lead and cement to stop it.

Special Effects: A few years after the death of Smith Treadwell, an exact likeness of him appeared on his gravestone.

Believe It or Not!®

The grave of composer Wolfgang Amadeus Mozart in St. Marx Cemetery, Vienna, Austria, is noteworthy because . . .

a. the tomb is still unfinished.
b. it contains no body.
c. it's shaped like a flute.
d. it's shaped like a harpsichord.

Dead Bolt: Lightning shattered the tombstone of T.G. Brownell, who was killed by a bolt of lightning.

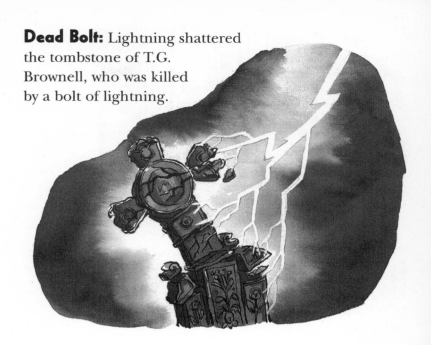

Miles to Go: In 1969, Miles Lucas of New Jersey was thrown from his car after it crashed into the wall of a cemetery. Lucas walked away from the accident, but his car kept going. It didn't stop until it finally landed on a headstone. The name of the headstone was Miles Lucas—no relation.

Lead Foot: Jonathan Blake's epitaph is a cautionary tale for speeders. It reads: Here lies the body of Jonathan Blake/Stepped on the gas instead of the brake.

HERE LIES
THE BODY OF
JONATHAN
BLAKE
STEPPED ON
THE GAS
INSTEAD OF
THE BRAKE

Last Act: In a strange and bizarre twist of fate Ripley himself would have appreciated, he collapsed in 1949 while making the 13th episode of his live weekly television series. The segment was a dramatized sequence on the origin of "Taps"—a hauntingly sad tune played at military funerals. Ripley died two days later and was buried in his hometown of Santa Rosa, California, in a place called Oddfellows Cemetery.

Believe It or Not!®

The Ripley Memorial, which was in a church in Santa Rosa, California, was made out of . . .

a. a two-ton slab of granite.
b. eight million matchsticks.
c. a single giant redwood tree.
d. five thousand roses, which are replaced every week.

Brain Buster

Straight from the crazy, mixed-up files of Mr. Robert L. Ripley, here are four facts that are just plain weird. Only catch is—one of them is totally made up. Can you figure out which one?

a. When Helen Jensen was a child, she swallowed a needle. Ouch! Thirty years later she found it in the thigh of her newborn baby.
Believe It!   **Not!**

b. A boy went to the doctor for a sore foot and found that a tooth was growing in his instep!
Believe It!   **Not!**

c. Brett Martin went to the doctor complaining of a severe earache only to find out that a pair of cockroaches was living in his inner ear.
Believe It!   **Not!**

d. A man came out of the hospital after recovering from a stroke and suddenly began speaking with a Scandinavian accent.
Believe It!   **Not!**

BONUS QUESTION

The book containing the transcript of the 1828 trial in which William Corder was convicted of murder can be seen in Moyses Hall Museum in Bury Saint Edmunds, England. What's so special about this book?

a. The text is written in Corder's own blood.

b. The text is bound in Corder's own skin.

c. The text glows bright red each year on the anniversary of Corder's trial.

POP QUIZ

Don't even think about closing this book! The Ripley's Brain Busters are not over yet. How much Creepy Stuff has stuck in your brain? How much raw Ripley's knowledge have you gained? It's time to find out! Circle your answers and give yourself five points for each question you answer correctly.

1. Which of the following is *not* an example of the sixth sense known as ESP?
a. A woman who can predict the outcome of court trials
b. A young girl who has a vision about the death of her pet before it happens
c. A woman who can name the ingredients of any perfume she smells
d. A woman who can run her hands over a map and point to places where oil will be found

2. Animals have amazing "sixth senses" of their own. After a man was killed while crossing the railroad tracks, Harry Goodman's dog would howl with fear whenever they approached the scene of the accident—even though the dog had not been there when the accident took place!
Believe It!   Not!

3. Which of the following is *not* believed by followers of astrology to affect the outcome of a person's life ?
a. The full moon.
b. The time, day, and month a person was born.
c. The position of furniture and other possessions in a room.

4. Which of the following strange coincidences is *not* true?
a. The Ebbins brothers from Bermuda died one year apart after being hit by the same taxicab driven by the same driver, carrying the same passenger.
b. George McDaniels and his father, mother, sister, two brothers, and an uncle all have the same birthday.
c. Kathy Moriarty and her seven sisters all had identical birthmarks in the exact same spot. Each sister has a crescent-shaped mole in the middle of her left cheek.

5. In the early 1900s, Harvey Lake, a conductor on a New Jersey train, made a big impression on the artistic director of the Academy of Music when he sang out the destinations in a beautiful tenor voice. The director immediately offered Lake a job as the star tenor in the New York City Opera.

Believe It!   Not!

6. Which of the following is *not* a link between Abraham Lincoln and John F. Kennedy?
a. They were both shot on a Friday.
b. Each one's wife was present when he was shot.
c. They were both shot in a theater.

7. Which of the following objects is *not* believed to be cursed?
a. The Hope Diamond
b. The automobile in which James Dean died
c. The car in which John F. Kennedy was assassinated
d. The tomb of Tutankhamen, who was the pharaoh of Egypt from 1361 to 1352 B.C.

8. The ancient Egyptians believed that a person's spirit returned to his or her body after death. They also believed that to open a tomb was to offend the gods and bring a curse upon oneself.
Believe It!   **Not!**

9. Henry Wadsworth Longfellow's poem, *"The Phantom Ship,"* is about . . .
a. a ship that disappeared in 1647 and appeared as a vision in the sky a year later.
b. the *Titanic,* which was carrying an ancient Egyptian mummy when it sank.
c. a Mississippi riverboat that sank after only three trips. Its engines were installed in four other ships. Three sank, and one was destroyed by fire.

10. Which of the following is *not* a place where ghosts have been spotted according to the records of Robert Ripley?
a. The White House
b. The elementary school attended by former President Bill Clinton
c. The Tower of London
d. The Burnley School of Professional Art in Seattle, Washington

11. Which of the following former U.S. presidents is *not* believed by some to still haunt the White House?
a. Abraham Lincoln
b. Andrew Jackson
c. Richard M. Nixon

12. Three unrelated men named Charles Fairwell were the only survivors of three different airplane crashes in 1942, 1964, and 1985.

Believe It!   **Not!**

13. The Jivaro headhunters of the Amazon often shrunk the heads of men. Women escaped being victims—at least until the early 1900s, when the upper bodies of women were often prepared for sale to tourists.

Believe It!   **Not!**

14. Which of the following is *not* used to predict the future?
a. Chiromancy
b. Astrology
c. Numerology
d. Paleontology

15. The bust of King Louis IX in the Sainte Chapelle church in Paris, France, is amazing because . . .
a. the nose on the bust is Louis's actual preserved nose.
b. a piece of Louis's skull lies beneath the crown on the sculpture's head.
c. strands of Louis's hair, eyelashes, and eyebrows are affixed to the sculpture.

Answer Key

Chapter 1

Believe It or Not!

Page 97:   **a.** precognition.
Page 99:   **d.** extrasensory perception.
Page 101:   **c.** Lyndon B. Johnson
Page 103:   **c.** Nostradamus.
Page 105:   **b.** the moon is full.
Page 107:   **b.** his own death from natural causes.
Page 109:   **c.** Theodore Roosevelt.
Page 111:   **c.** In India.
Page 112:   **b.** it snowed three times.
Brain Buster: a. is false.
Bonus Question: c.

Chapter 2

Believe It or Not!

Page 115:   **d.** George Washington.
Page 116:   **a.** pants zipper.
Page 119:   **a.** Gemini.
Page 121:   **b.** Harry S Truman.
Page 123:   **a.** 13th floor.
Page 125:   **c.** by another Claude Volbonne who was
             unrelated to his father's murderer.
Page 126:   **b.** Bermuda Triangle.
Brain Buster: b. is false.
Bonus Question: b.

Chapter 3

Believe It or Not!

Page 129:   **a.** died within a year.

Page 130:   **d.** bolt of lightning.

Page 133:   **a.** wore the same helmet.

Page 135:   **d.** mummies.

Page 137:   **b.** *Hesperus."*

Page 138:   **b.** it toppled over, crushing
Caffa to death.

Brain Buster: **a.** is false.

Bonus Question: a.

Chapter 4

Believe It or Not!

Page 141:   **d.** Robert E. Lee.

Page 143:   **d.** The Tower of London

Page 145:   **a.** Headless Nellie.

Page 146:   **d.** Sons of Witches.

Page 148:   **a.** rooster for laying an egg?

Brain Buster: **d.** is false.

Bonus Question: b.

Chapter 5

Believe It or Not!

Page 151: **b.** middle finger.

Page 153: **c.** died of fright.

Page 154: **a.** the palm of their hand.

Page 157: **a.** human skull.

Page 158: **b.** that love can outlast death.

Page 161: **a.** allowing five candles on each outstretched arm to burn down to the flesh.

Page 162: **b.** it contains no body.

Page 164: **c.** a single giant redwood tree.

Brain Buster: c. is false.

Bonus Question: b.

Pop Quiz

1. **c.**
2. **Believe It!**
3. **c.**
4. **c.**
5. **Not!**
6. **c.**
7. **c.**
8. **Believe It!**
9. **a.**
10. **b.**
11. **c.**
12. **Not!**
13. **Believe It!**
14. **d.**
15. **b.**

What's Your Ripley's Rank?

Ripley's Scorecard

Congrats! You've busted your brain on some crazy, creepy facts and challenged your ability to tell fact from fiction. Now it's time to rate your Ripley's knowledge. Are you a Spooky Superstar or a Ripley's Realist? Check out the answers in the answer key and use this page to keep track of how many trivia questions you've answered correctly. Then add 'em up and find out how you rate.

Here's the scoring breakdown—give yourself:
★ **10 points** for every **Believe It or Not!** you answered correctly;

★ **20 points** for every fiction you spotted in the **Ripley's Brain Busters**;

★ **10** for every **Bonus Question** you answered right;

★ and **5** for every **Pop Quiz** question you answered correctly.

Here's a tally sheet:
Number of **Believe It or Not!** questions answered correctly:	_____ x 10 =	_____
Number of **Ripley's Brain Buster** questions answered correctly:	_____ x 20 =	_____
Number of **Bonus Questions** answered correctly:	_____ x 10 =	_____
Chapter Total:		_____

Write your totals for each chapter and the Pop Quiz section in the spaces below. Then add them up to get your FINAL SCORE. Your FINAL SCORE decides how you rate:

Chapter One Total: _____

Chapter Two Total: _____

Chapter Three Total _____

Chapter Four Total: _____

Chapter Five Total: _____

Pop Quiz Total: _____

FINAL SCORE: _____

525–301
Spooky Superstar

You are eerily excellent. You've got a sixth sense for the spooky and a gripping grasp on the gory. Your Ripley's know-how is top-notch. Nothing creeps you out. And nothing gets past you—you can spot a fantasy-fact miles away! Your ability to tell fact from fiction is out of the ordinary and unbelievably amazing. You are a force to be reckoned with. Keep up the good work!

300-201
Amazing Ace

You are creeping your way up to the top of the ranks. You know a true tale when you see one—spooky or not. And your sense for the suspicious is supercharged. You're no sucker for a made-up ghost story or a tall tale, but you find yourself getting carried away once in a while. That's okay! Go with your gut—you've got superstar potential.

200-101
Creepy Convert

Your eye for the eerie is getting better. But the mere thought of the dead coming back to life or a ghost in the attic sends chills down your spine. You may not be totally gullible, but it's fairly easy to trick you with a phony fact or made-up mystery. If "seeing is believing," you tend to believe what you read. Keep working on your sixth sense—you'll be amazed by what you can do.

100-0
Ripley's Realist

You're a down-to-earth, believe-it-when-you-see-it kind of person. Sure, you may not pay enough attention to tales of ghosts, goblins, witches, or even superstitions to be able to spot the fiction among the facts, but you like it that way. And while you totally get that truth can be stranger than fiction, your no-nonsense attitude helps you deal with anything remotely out of the ordinary. Case closed.

Photo Credits

Ripley Entertainment Inc. and the editors of this book wish to thank the following photographers, agents, and other individuals for permission to use and reprint the following photographs in this book. Any photographs included in this book that are not acknowledged below are property of the Ripley Archives. Great effort has been made to obtain permission from the owners of all materials included in this book. Any errors that may have been made are unintentional and will gladly be corrected in future printings if notice is sent to Ripley Entertainment Inc., 5728 Major Boulevard, Orlando, Florida 32819.

98 Franklin D. Roosevelt; 111 King George III; 121 Lightning/CORBIS

98 Warren G. Harding; 101 William Blake; 112 Bust of Julius Caesar; 130 Archduke Ferdinand; 136 Tamerlane; 143 Catherine Howard/Bettmann/CORBIS

99 Jeanne Dixon/Associated Press UNIVERSAL PRESS SYNDICATE

101 General MacArthur and Troops; 118 Mark Newman and Jerry Levey; 114 Brian Epstein/Associated Press

103 Fire; 107 Oil Rig; 123 Apple/Copyright Ripley Entertainment and its licensors

105 Chris Robinson/Chris Robinson

112 *The Old Farmer's Almanac*/ www.almanac.com

117 Mel Gibson/Rogers & Cohen

123 Black Cat/Santokh Kochar/PhotoDisc

124 Abraham Lincoln/Library of Congress, Prints and Photographs Division, LC-USZ62-13016 DLC

98, 124 John F. Kennedy/Photo No. ST-C237-1-63 in the John F. Kennedy Library

126 Dalai Lama/Galen Rowell/CORBIS

126 Shipwreck/Mark Downey/PhotoDisc

129 Hope Diamond/Smithsonian Institution

135 Tutankhamen's Tomb/Hulton-Deutsch Collection Limited/CORBIS

141 Mary Todd Lincoln/The Lloyd Ostendorf Collection

142 Andrew Jackson/Library of Congress, Prints and Photographs Division, LC-USZ62-5099 DLC

146 Johannesburg Castle/Franziska Oelmann

155 Hangman's Rope/Laura Miller

156 Sainte Chapelle/The Paris Pages

157 Bone Church/Ben Fraser

160 Fragonard Sculpture/C. Degueurce

Contents

Introduction

The Odd-inary World of Robert Ripley

Robert Ripley was the first cartoonist in history to become a millionaire. The "Indiana Jones" of his time, he traveled all over the world, looking for amazing facts, oddities, and curiosities. Ripley delighted in learning about the customs of the people who lived in the countries he visited. When he returned home, he would often tell their stories in his Believe It or Not! cartoons.

An avid people watcher, Ripley captured his subjects in countless photographs. He was especially intrigued by those people whose physical appearance varied from the norm. Many of these human oddities appeared in person at Ripley's Odditoriums. Others were cast in wax and can still be seen in Odditoriums, museums of the fascinating and bizarre, all over the world.

Robert Ripley opened his first Odditorium at the 1933 Chicago World's Fair, A Century of Progress International Exposition. More than two million people passed through its doors, making it one of the most popular exhibits. People fainted at the sight of contortionists, magicians, eye-poppers, fireproof people,

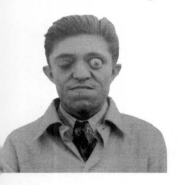

and razor-blade eaters—but that did not stop them from coming back for more!

The first Odditorium was such a success that Ripley opened other Odditoriums in Cleveland, San Diego, Dallas, San Francisco, and New York. Like the first one, they were all hugely successful, featuring such people pleasers as vaudeville artists, contortionists, and odd-looking people of all shapes and sizes.

No one dared use the word "freak" in the presence of Robert Ripley. He had a deep regard for the unusual people who performed in his Odditoriums, and he expected everyone else to show them the same respect he did. Knowing that they would be treated well, performance artists flocked to Ripley's door from far and wide—a man who could swallow a mouse and cough it up unharmed from his stomach, a one-legged tap dancer, a man who could talk with his mouth full of billiard balls. There was even a man who could turn his head around 180 degrees and look directly behind himself.

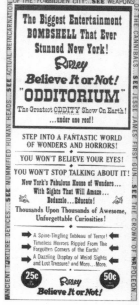

In the following pages you'll meet unusual people from all over the world. You can also test your "stranger than fiction" smarts by taking the Would You Believe? quizzes and solving the Brain Buster in each chapter. Then you can try the special Pop Quiz at the end of the book and use the scorecard to find out your Ripley's Rank.

So get ready to enter the world of men, women, and children from the past and present whose uniqueness is bound to amaze you.

Believe It!®

Some unusual-looking people are born with unique features, but others go to great lengths to achieve the bizarre look they want.

Omi, Oh, My! An English military officer in World War I, the Great Omi sported tattoos from the top of his head to the bottom of his feet. It took 15 million needle stabs to do the job.

Would You Believe?

An 18th-century Englishman named Thomas Wedders had a 7.5-inch long . . .

a. big toe.
b. nose.
c. earlobe.
d. little finger.

Messie Hair: French actor Pierre Messie could move his hair at will, causing it to stand, fall, or curl. He could even curl one side while leaving the other straight. What accounted for this ability? Messie may have had unusually well-developed muscles in his hair follicles. This trait is common in some animal species but is rare in human beings.

189

On File: In 1974, Renda Long of Glendale, Arizona, started growing her fingernails. By 1985, her longest nail had reached 14.5 inches while the shortest was a mere 8.5 inches.

Hair to There: One-time holder of the world's record, Lydia McPherson's red hair eventually grew to a length of seven feet four inches.

Would You Believe?

In 1937 at the Cleveland Odditorium, Johnny Eck was billed as the "most remarkable man" alive because he was born with . . .

a. two noses.
b. hooves instead of feet.
c. only half a body.
d. a transparent body.

Reptile Man:

Erik Sprague of Albany, New York, had himself tattooed with scales from head to toe. These, along with his surgically split tongue and the bony ridge that was set into his forehead, make him look like a reptile.

Quadruple Pupil: Liu Ch'ung of Shansi, China, was born in A.D. 955 with two pupils in each eye. His unusual

anatomy did not keep him from having a successful political career as governor of Shansi and minister of state. Ch'ung was one of Ripley's all-time favorite "human oddities" and is one of the most popular wax figures in a number of Ripley's Odditoriums.

Bearded Wonder: Edwin Smith, a miner during the mid-1800s California gold rush, liked his beard so much, he let it grow for 16 years. It reached a length of eight feet—so long that Smith had to hire a servant just to wash and comb it!

Hairy Problem: A rare condition called hypertrichosis, also known as "werewolf syndrome," causes uncontrolled hair growth. Jo Jo the Dog-Faced Boy, who suffered from the condition, was a popular circus performer in the 1880s. Today, brothers Larry and Danny Gomez, who live near Guadalajara, Mexico, have found a way to capitalize on their condition. They call themselves the Wolf Brothers and are known all over the world for their skill as trapeze artists.

The Human Unicorn: In 1928, Ripley found a photograph of a Manchurian farmer known only as Weng, who had a 13-inch horn on the back of his head.

Lighting the Way: In 1923, Ripley met a man in Chunking, China, who had a hole in his head. Known as Lighthouse Man, he made good use of the hole by sticking a candle into it and using the light to guide visitors around dark city streets.

Left Again and Again: Every male in the Colombière family of Nancy, France, was born with two left hands. The men were perfectly normal in every way except that both of their hands had thumbs on the right side.

Would You Believe?

Pogonophobia is the scientific term for a fear of . . .

a. beards.
b. long fingernails.
c. tattoos.
d. red hair.

Above It All:

Born in 1918, Robert Wadlow of Alton, Illinois, grew to a height of eight feet eleven inches. In order for him to ride in the family car, the front passenger seat had to be removed to allow room for his long legs. A kind and generous soul, Wadlow was dubbed "the gentle giant" by the people of his hometown.

Tallboy: Igor Ladan of Russia stood six feet tall when he was seven years old.

Diaper Service: During the French Revolution, Monsieur Richebourg, who at 21 was the size of a two-year-old, was a spy for the Royalists. He smuggled information through enemy lines by posing as a baby and concealing the messages in his diapers.

Little Big Man: Though he weighed a whopping nine pounds two ounces at birth, Tom Thumb never grew beyond three feet four inches tall. But that did not keep him from becoming one of the biggest celebrities of his time. In the 1860s, Thumb was received by the queens of England, France, Spain, and Belgium, and his fame helped him amass an immense fortune. He married Lavinia Warren in 1863 in a ceremony attended by dignitaries from all over the world. The reception featured a wedding cake that weighed 80 pounds—more than the bride and groom combined. The tiny couple settled in Connecticut, where they acquired a mansion filled with antique furniture—all miniaturized, of course.

Would You Believe?

Colon T. Updike was known as "the human horse" because he had . . .

a. hair too thick to cut.
b. a taste for oats and hay.
c. a hairy 18-inch-long mane.
d. hooves.

195

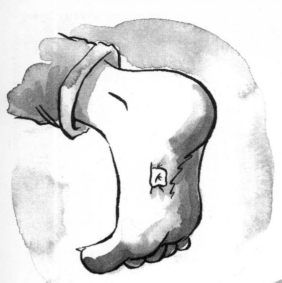

Nothing but the Tooth:
In 1978, Doug Pritchard, age 13, of Lenoir, North Carolina, went to his doctor with a sore foot. The diagnosis? There was a tooth growing in the bottom of his instep!

More to Love:
This baby, born in 1936, weighed 92 pounds at the age of six months.

Big Foot:
In 1999, Nike made the first size 23 sneaker especially for Brad Millard of St. Mary's College in California. This is the largest size sneaker Nike has ever made—even larger than Shaquille O'Neal's, which is a mere size 22. Millard's basketball coach jokes, "When Brad gets a new pair of sneakers, I take the box home and use it as an extra bedroom."

Tall Story: Born in the mid-1800s, Anna Swan of Canada was as tall as her mother by the age of six. At 14, she was a foot taller than her father. She finally stopped growing at seven feet five and one-half inches. After a short career in P. T. Barnum's museum, Swan set sail for Europe. On the ship, she met and fell in love with Captain Martin Van Buren Bates of the Confederate cavalry. Just slightly shorter than Swan, the captain came from a long line of giants and was still growing at the age of 24. The couple married and settled in Ohio, where they built an 18-room house with 14-foot-high ceilings. All their furniture was giant-sized— even Anna's grand piano, which was mounted on three-foot stilts. In 1873, the couple had a baby boy, who weighed a strapping 23.5 pounds at birth.

Would You Believe?

Adam Rainer, born in Austria in 1899, stood three feet ten inches when he was 21. Yet when he died at the age of 51, he was . . .

a. six feet ten inches.
b. three feet four inches.
c. seven feet eight inches.
d. five feet nine inches.

Tooth or Dare: During the Middle Ages, fashionable women in Japan blackened their teeth to make themselves attractive to others.

Anatomically Incorrect: Long-necked women are considered beautiful by the Padaung people of Myanmar (formerly Burma). To achieve this look, a female is fitted with a metal necklace in early childhood. More necklace rings are added as she grows until the neck has been stretched to the desired length. The catch? The rings must be worn for life.

Queen of De Nile: Elizabeth Christensen, 39-year-old wife and mother, believes she is the reincarnation of Queen Nefertiti, who lived over 3,000 years ago. Christensen has spent $250,000 on 240 operations to sculpt her face into a likeness of the Egyptian queen (*see color insert*).

Lip Service: In the past, women of the Sara people of Chad, Africa, tried to make themselves unattractive to slave raiders. In childhood, a girl's lips were pierced and wooden plates inserted. The size of the plates was gradually increased. Eventually, the lower lip was stretched enough that a 14-inch plate could be worn.

Tri-lingual: Edward Bovington was born in Burnham, England, in the 16th century with two eyes, one nose, and one mouth—but three tongues.

Would You Believe?

For many years, every single person in Cervera de Buitrago, Spain, was born with . . .

a. two left feet.
b. only one eye.
c. no fingernails or toenails.
d. six fingers on each hand.

199

Eggs-aggerated Headlines:

During the early 20th century, the Mangbetu people of Central Africa considered elongated skulls a sign of beauty and intelligence. To achieve this highly desirable shape, they bound the heads of infants. In adulthood, both men and women wore hats or wrapped their hair around baskets to make the head look even longer.

Catwoman:

Socialite Jocelyne Wildenstein is also known as the "Bride of Wildenstein" because she's had so much plastic surgery. Why? Because she wanted to look like one of the cats in her billionaire husband's private jungle.

Would You Believe?

For a time during the reign of Louis XIV of France, it was the fashion to bind a young girl's head with laces in order to form long ridges in her scalp that could . . .

a. support the three-foot-tall hairstyles of the day.
b. hold hair jewels securely.
c. support many layers of braids.
d. securely hold several yards of ribbon.

Sometimes fact is stranger than fiction. Are you ready to test your knowledge of odd human behavior, crazy customs, and super-strange skills?

The Ripley files are packed with info that's too out-there to believe. Each shocking oddity proves that truth is stranger than fiction. But it takes a keen eye, a sharp mind, and good instincts to spot the difference. Can you handle it?

Each Ripley's Brain Buster contains a group of four unbelievably strange statements. In each group only **one** is **false**. Read each extra-odd entry and circle whether you **Believe It!** or **Not!** And if you're up to the challenge, take on the bonus question in each section and the Pop Quiz at the end of the book. Then flip to the Answer Key, keep track of your score, and rate your skills.

Sometimes what's strangest about people isn't their odd behavior or the funny ways in which they alter their appearance—it's the human body itself. Which one of these bizarre body facts is completely false?

a. There are 625 sweat glands in each square inch of your skin.

Believe It!   **Not!**

b. By the time you reach the age of 70, you will have shed 40 pounds of skin.

Believe It!   **Not!**

c. Taste is the only one of the five senses with a direct connection to the brain. It's also closest to the parts of the brain that trigger memories and emotions. That's why one taste of something can bring on a flood of memories.

Believe It!   **Not!**

d. A person blinks an average of 84,000,000 times a year!

Believe It!   **Not!**

• •

BONUS QUESTION

Some people will try anything! A dogmobile was patented in the United States in 1870. What did it do?

a. It provided motorized transportation for dogs that could no longer walk.

b. It provided front-wheel drive by means of two dogs running inside a cage in the front wheels.

c. It used dogs instead of horses to pull small carriages.

Get ready to meet a group of people whose superhuman powers of memory, daring, or physical strength are phenomenal.

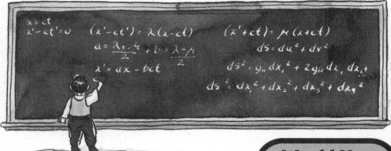

No Problem: At the age of four, Ung-Young Kim of Seoul, South Korea, could solve mathematical problems based on Einstein's theory of relativity.

Baby Tape Recorder: Murasaki Shikibu had such a remarkable memory that, at the age of two, she could repeat 1,000 lines of poetry after having heard them just once.

Would You Believe?

At the age of five, little Louis Miller of Philadelphia . . .

a. got his black belt in karate.
b. composed his first opera.
c. was accepted at the University of Pennsylvania.
d. spoke eight languages.

Gravely Unsettling: Nicholas Settle of Nyack, New York, could walk through any cemetery once, then recite the epitaphs on each tombstone from memory.

Little Professor: Jean-Philippe Bratier (1721–1740) spoke German, French, and Latin at the age of four, translated the Greek Bible at age five, and read Hebrew at age six.

Fully Committed: Elijah, the Gaon, chief rabbi of Lithuania, committed 2,500 books, including the Bible and the Talmud, to memory, and could repeat any passage from them at will.

Would You Believe?

Guy Mitchell of Iowa passed the Morse code test for his radio operator's license . . .

a. at the age of four.
b. without studying.
c. on his tenth birthday.
d. by using sign language.

Mad Professor: The Oxford English Dictionary was begun in London in 1878 under the editorship of Professor James Murray, who solicited entries from volunteers. One volunteer, American Army surgeon Dr. William Charles Minor, who had served in the Civil War, was responsible for about 10,000 entries. Murray was so impressed by Minor's scholarship that he repeatedly invited Minor to visit him. But Minor never accepted. The reason? He was an inmate in the Broadmoor Hospital for the Criminally Insane, where he had been confined in 1871 for killing a man while in a deluded state.

Most Noteworthy: Musician and composer Wolfgang Amadeus Mozart (1756–1791) could listen to a symphony by another composer once, then write it down, note for note.

Early Learning: English economist and philosopher John Stuart Mill learned Greek at the age of three. By the time he was eight, he also knew Latin, which he taught to his sister.

Fun with Numbers: Savant Paul Erdös was a brilliant mathematician, but when it came to day-to-day living, he was mentally, physically, and socially challenged. Just opening a simple container could pose a major problem for him. Once he stabbed a can of juice with a pair of scissors, spilling the contents all over the floor. Though Erdös was the most published mathematician of all time, he could not even tie his own shoelaces! Erdös rarely bathed or changed his clothes, but he was warmly welcomed by many world-class mathematicians, who were eager to bask in the light of his genius.

Word Perfect:

Jack Fletcher of Wargrave, England, was considered the "village idiot," yet he could quote every sermon he heard in any of ten nearby churches word for word, giving a perfect imitation of each preacher's voice and delivery.

Large Hard Drive:

The savant Kim Peek, inspiration for the film *Rain Man*, read his first book at the age of 16 months. Peek has a brain that is one-third larger than normal. Because there is no separation, or filtering mechanism, between the left and right sides of his brain, it saves every piece of information it receives.

Perhaps this is why Peek can not only tell you the day of the week for any date in history, but can also recall every word of the more than 8,000 books he's read so far.

Would You Believe?

England's King George III (1738–1820) could recite from memory . . .

a. the titles of all 2,500 books in his castle library.

b. the 10,000 virtues required of a king.

c. the complete works of St. Augustine—containing eight million words.

d. the names of all 4,500 officers in the British Navy and the ship to which each was assigned.

Well Balanced: In 1953, 148-pound Bob Dotzauer balanced three lawnmowers on his chin—which, combined, weighed five pounds more than he did.

Human Bridge: Eighteenth-century strongman Thomas Topham of Derby, England, could lie suspended between two stools and lift a six-foot-long table with his teeth while four men stood on his body.

Nice Kitty: German circus performer Miss Heliot entertained audiences in 1953 by carrying a 660-pound lion on her shoulders.

Would You Believe?

In 1979, John Massis of Belgium prevented a helicopter from taking off, using a rope and harness held . . .

a. between two fingers.
b. in his teeth.
c. around his neck.
d. in his clenched fists.

Strong-arm Tactic: Allen Durwood, bodyguard to King Malcolm McAnmore of Scotland, was so strong he was able to keep 20 assassins from entering the castle by holding the door closed with just one arm.

Tiny Chairman:

At the age of five months, Victor Casados, Jr., could simultaneously lift two chairs weighing nine pounds each.

Uplifting Performance:

In the 18th century, Miss Darnett, known as "The Singing Strong Lady," sang a song while supporting a platform that held the pianist and his piano.

Supportive Husband:

In the late 1890s, famous Canadian strongman Louis Cyr supported his 125-pound wife as she climbed a ladder that he held in one outstretched hand.

Pulling a Fast One: Kevin Fast was nicknamed "Bench" in college because he could bench press 500 pounds. Since then, he's been inspired to try something no one's attempted before—pulling two giant fire engines. It normally takes seven men to move just one fire engine, but Fast was able to move both!

Heavy Load: Len Ashton, a South African circus performer, can balance heavy objects on his chin—such as a lawn mower, his three-year-old son seated on a chair, and a washing machine.

Would You Believe?

In 1990, Malaysian strongman R. Letchemanah pulled a Boeing 737 airplane 50 feet with his . . .

a. right arm.
b. little finger.
c. hair.
d. leg.

Hot Feat: On August 2, 1938, people gasped in astonishment as they watched Kuda Bux of India walk through fire. A ditch 20 feet long, three feet wide, and four

feet deep outside of Radio City Music Hall in New York City had been filled with a layer of fiery coals. Twenty-four hours later, the temperature inside the pit had reached more than 1,200°F. After walking the length of the ditch through the hot coals barefoot up to his ankles, Bux was examined by doctors, who found no injuries.

Helping Hands: Master Zhou is an expert in a Chinese art called Tchi Gong, which uses energy to heal. The energy that flows through Zhou's hands has been recorded at 202°F. Zhou begins treatment with what looks like a simple massage. Then he wraps a piece of tin foil inside a moistened paper towel and places it on the patient's chest. As he passes his hands over it, steam rises from the paper towel. People who have had the treatment claim to feel more focused and full of energy. Others believe they have been cured of a variety of ailments from headaches to cancer.

Suspended Animation: In 1837, to demonstrate the power of meditation, a yogi named Haridas allowed himself to be buried alive for 40 days. In preparation for the ordeal, the mystic went into a self-induced trance. Before burying him, his assistants filled his ears, nose, and mouth with wax and wrapped him in a blanket. A guard was posted at his "grave" to make sure that no trickery took place. When the assistants dug Haridas up 40 days later, he was extremely thin but otherwise in perfect shape.

Would You Believe?

While lying on a bed of nails, yogi Zdenek Zahradka of Ústí nad Labem, Czech Republic, regularly . . .

a. practiced mental telepathy.
b. slept.
c. practiced yoga.
d. gave blood.

Over the Edge: Extreme kayaker Tao Berman was the first person to go over Johnston Canyon Waterfall at Banff National Park in Alberta, Canada. Equivalent to a jump from a ten-story building, the 98-foot drop is just eight feet wide at the top and lined on both sides with jagged rocks.

Leaps of Faith: The Land Divers of Pentecost, one of the islands of Vanuatu in the South Pacific, have been bungee-jumping for hundreds of years—but they use vines instead of bungee cords. The divers jump headfirst from an 80-foot-high tower.

The vines attached to their ankles slow their plunges, but each year, some divers are injured when the vines snap. Why do they do it? It's a coming-of-age ritual, with boys as young as eight making their first jump.

Respect Your Elders:

On December 10, 1997, Julia "Butterfly" Hill climbed 180 feet up an ancient redwood tree in a bold attempt to save a forest from being cut down. She did not come down for two years. Enclosed in a dome of multi-colored tarps, Hill lived on a tiny wooden platform, using a bucket for a toilet, candles for light, and a one-burner propane stove to cook on.

A ground crew brought her supplies, which she pulled up with ropes. During her record-breaking time in the tree, Hill endured 90-mile-per-hour winds and harassment by lumber company helicopters. She came down only when the company agreed to protect the surrounding three acres from logging.

Would You Believe?

Using only one finger, Mike Gooch of England performed 16 consecutive push-ups, balanced on a . . .

a. coconut.
b. merry-go-round.
c. seesaw.
d. Ping-Pong ball.

A Wheely Great Time: One of Canadian unicyclist Kris Holm's record-breaking stunts involved riding within four inches of a 2,000-foot cliff and leaping six feet across a crevasse thousands of feet deep—all without brakes and with nothing to hold on to.

Would You Believe?

Nature photographer Tony Hurtubise invented a suit 50 times stronger and 85 percent lighter than steel. To test it out, he . . .

a. was shot out of a cannon into a brick wall.
b. let a train run over him.
c. wrestled with a grizzly bear.
d. had a car suspended on wires swung into his chest like a pendulum.

Double-cross: The Adung River Bridge in Myanmar consists only of a 150-foot-long rope strung 40 feet above the water. Women with babies strapped to their backs haul themselves across the bridge while hanging upside down in a ring made of reeds.

How fine-tuned is your radar for the ridiculous? Figure out which one of the following four amazing abilities is too blatantly false to believe.

a. On his 80th birthday, Master Engineer Junior Grade Gardner A. Taylor lifted a 110-pound anvil that was suspended from his ears! His set his own lifetime record at age 64 when he lifted 175 pounds using ear power alone.
Believe It!   Not!

b. In the 1930s, George Bove of New York City claimed he could determine a person's gender by dangling a key on a piece of thread over a handwriting sample. And he was right every time!
Believe It!   Not!

c. In the 1980s, Gabrielle O'Mally became a legend at Ripley's Odditoriums around the nation by spinning her left foot 360 degrees on her ankle joint.
Believe It!   Not!

d. In June 1930, U.S. Navy wrestling champion Joe Reno was hypnotized and slept buried in a coffin for almost 17 days without food or water. But nothing could keep Joe down. Only 15 minutes after being awakened and released from the coffin, Joe wrestled middleweight champion Red Lindsay for ten minutes before the match was declared a tie.
Believe It!   Not!

BONUS QUESTION

What amazing feat did Lotte Frutiger of Allalinhorn, Switzerland, accomplish in 1927 when she was only eight years old?

a. She became the youngest person ever to hold the record for ice diving. She immersed herself in icy water for over 40 minutes!

b. She climbed Mount Allalinhorn, which is 13,234 feet high and always covered in ice.

c. She had herself buried alive in a block of ice and survived for 78 hours without food and water.

The following pages are filled with individuals who dare to be different in ways that most people would never even dream of.

Cat-echism: During the 16th century, England's Cardinal Wolsey (1475–1530) regularly took his cats to church.

Would You Believe?

German poet Friedrich von Schiller (1759–1805) could only compose poetry while sitting . . .

a. with his parakeet on his head.
b. in his pajamas.
c. with his cat in his lap.
d. with his feet in ice water.

Chilling Performance: During the 1939 World's Fair, performance artist Annetta Del Mar of Chicago, Illinois, had her body entirely frozen and thawed up to 30 times a day.

Junk Food: Michel Lotito, long considered a medical mystery, found that his unusual ability to chew and swallow indigestible household objects such as razor blades, nuts, bolts, china, glasses, and cutlery could be parlayed into a career. To date, he has ingested a grocery cart, a bicycle, a coffin, and a complete Cessna airplane.

Riveting Performance: In the 1970s, Bill Steed, a professor of frog psychology at Croaker College, used hypnosis to train frogs to perform amazing feats such as lifting barbells.

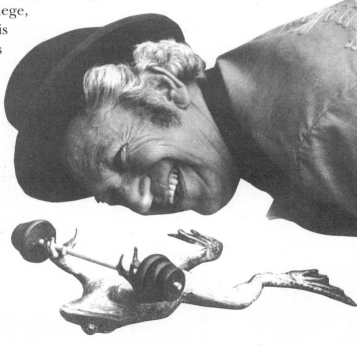

Tummy Tuck:

Alfred Hitchcock, the famous film director of movies such as *Psycho* and *The Birds,* thought belly buttons were ugly. So he had his own surgically removed.

Beastly Welcome:

Writer and naturalist Charles Waterton (1782–1864) sometimes slept outside with a tree-dwelling mammal called a sloth. He was also known to act like a dog, greet his guests with a growl, and scratch his head with his big toe.

Would You Believe?

King Henry II of France suffered from ailurophobia, a terrible fear of . . .

a. snakes.
b. birds.
c. cats.
d. bees.

Suit Sower: One day the seed of an idea for a new act popped into performance artist Gene Pool's head. Why not grow a suit out of grass and then get chased by a lawn mower? He did just that and, in the process, discovered that he had a green thumb. Not one to let the grass grow under his feet, Pool started his own clothing line and has perfected his art to the point where he can grow an entire three-piece suit in just two weeks. Grass-covered cars are another of his specialties.

Fowl Fashion: During the 1700s, Ignatz Von Roll, a turkey farmer in Germany, had all of his birds fitted with tiny Turkish turbans.

Cornball Gown: In 1947, Virginia Winn of Mercedes, Texas, stitched 60,000 grains of corn onto an evening dress. The completed gown weighed 40 pounds.

All the News That's Fit to Wear: It took Mrs. Willis N. Ward and Mrs. J. Hoppemath the better part of 1939 to make their newsprint coats.

All Buttoned Up: In 1936, Owen Totten of Mt. Erie, Illinois, modeled a suit he'd covered with 5,600 buttons—no two of which were alike.

Would You Believe?

Bill Black of St. Louis, Missouri, started an entire line of clothing made of . . .

a. ostrich feathers.
b. human hair.
c. seashells.
d. moss.

A Dog's Life: The eighth Earl of Bridgewater, who died in 1829, dressed his dogs in fine clothing and allowed them to eat dinner at his table every day.

Gem of a Meal: King Henry III of France, who ruled from 1574 to 1589, dined regularly on partridges coated with solid gold, omelets sprinkled with ground-up pearls, and poultry soaked in expensive perfume.

Puppy Love: France's King Henry III was also so fond of pets that whenever his favorite dog had a litter, he'd carry the puppies for days in a basket slung from his neck.

Lovebirds: To appease the gods, Khanderav, ruler of Baroda, India, from 1856 to 1870, spent $200,000 to host 42 marriage ceremonies. In each case, the bride and groom were pigeons.

Had Their Cake and Heard It, Too:

In 1533, at the wedding of the Duke of Orléans (who became Henry II of France) and Catherine de Médicis, a four-piece orchestra played to the guests from inside a huge wedding cake.

Would You Believe?

To improve their studies, schoolboys in Morocco are fed . . .

a. ground toadstools.
b. shark eyeballs.
c. salmon tails.
d. hedgehog livers.

Caveman Chic:

During the 18th century, Charles Hamilton, a wealthy eccentric, paid a hermit $700 to live in a cave in his garden.

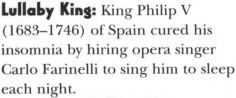

Worth His Salt:

American millionaire Alfred Gwynne Vanderbilt was so superstitious that he slept with the legs of his bed set in dishes of salt.

Lullaby King: King Philip V

(1683–1746) of Spain cured his insomnia by hiring opera singer Carlo Farinelli to sing him to sleep each night.

Would You Believe?

King Louis XIV of France regularly washed only the tip of his nose because . . .

a. of the low water supply.
b. he was afraid of water.
c. of his religious beliefs.
d. he hated the taste of water.

Wedding Costume: Allen Roulston and Linda MacLaggan of Toronto, Canada, dressed up as Frankenstein and the Bride of Frankenstein for their Halloween Day wedding.

Lionhearted: French actor Charles Dullin (1885–1949) spent several years training for the stage by reciting poetry daily while inside a cage filled with lions.

Through the Roof:

American financier J. Pierpont Morgan was so committed to wearing extra-high silk top hats that he ordered high-roofed limousines custom-built for himself.

Fowl Balls:

In 1989, a group of grocery store clerks in Newport, California, formed an unofficial bowling league called the Poultry Association. Using frozen turkeys as bowling balls and one-liter soft-drink bottles as pins, they bowled to raise money for charity.

Captive Audience:

The faithful widow Countess Antoinette de Bethune Pologne kept her husband's skull on her desk and read to it from his favorite two books every day for 25 years.

Horsing Around:

In the 19th century, Jonathan James Toogood from Overblow, England, regularly jumped his horse over hedges while riding backward.

Would You Believe?

The French poet Charles Baudelaire (1821–1867) walked through the parks of Paris . . .

a. wearing only his bathrobe.
b. with a parrot on his shoulder.
c. with a lobster on a leash.
d. with a mouse in his pocket.

Dirty Trick:

In the 1930s in Howe, Indiana, a woman, known locally as the "Animal Woman," lived with skunks and did not bathe or change her clothes for 25 years. As if to prove the wisdom of her lifestyle, she died ten days after she was given her first bath.

Major Tantrum:

When his parents refused to buy him a motorcycle, Dan Jaimun of Bangkok, Thailand, locked himself in his room and stayed there for 22 years.

Señor Lancelot:

Juanito Apiñani, a 19th-century Spanish matador, thrilled crowds by using a lance to leap over charging bulls.

Would You Believe?

Every morning before British poet Edith Sitwell began to work she . . .

a. took a bath in a tub of milk.
b. ate a dozen pancakes with jam.
c. lay in an open coffin.
d. fed her 60 pet cockatiels.

High-tech Howard:

In 1938, millionaire Howard Hughes set a round-the-world speed record, flying at 352.39 miles per hour in a plane that was filled with Ping-Pong balls. He took the balls along so they would cushion his fall and keep him afloat in case he crashed into the ocean.

The following people could ace a talent competition any day. Can you pick out which twisted talent is not real?

a. Ruwan Jayatilleke of Englewood, New Jersey, can shoot peas out of his nose at speeds of up to 30 miles per hour.
Believe It!   Not!

b. At only three and a half months old, Ted Elbert Carmack could lift his own weight on a chin-up bar.
Believe It!   Not!

c. In the 1940s, Alan Cooke of Baltimore, Maryland, could eat, sleep, and drink while floating in water. To prove that he wouldn't sink, he was thrown tied, taped, and bound into the Chesapeake Bay 15 times, into Lake Michigan, and into various rivers and indoor pools. He floated to the surface every time!
Believe It!   Not!

d. On December 4, 1934, Forrest Yanky lassoed a housefly with a piece of thread while his entire family watched in awe.
Believe It!   Not!

●●

BONUS QUESTION

What made poet Emily Dickinson (1830–1903) a little out of the ordinary?

a. She never wrote down a single word on paper. Instead, she committed each of her poems to memory and recited them to her circle of friends.

b. She had a constant headache for 26 years, yet never missed a day of writing.

c. She thought she was so ugly, she would stay in another room whenever she had visitors and talk to them through an open door.

CHAPTER 4 Weird Ways

Things that seem perfectly natural to some people may seem downright strange to others.

Balancing Act:

Women of the Balanta tribe in Binnar, Guinea-Bissau, Africa, annually perform a dance in which they balance a huge basket containing their sweetheart or husband on their head.

Would You Believe?

For a month after his wedding, an African Masai bridegroom must . . .

a. do all the cooking.
b. wear his wife's clothing.
c. obey his mother-in-law.
d. wash all the dishes.

H₂0 for K9s:

A supermarket in Blackhawk, California, sells Thirsty Pup, a bottled water for dogs.

Nature's Night-lights: One of the world's oldest plants, the puya raimondi, grows in the Cordillera Mountains of Peru. These plants feature a shaft of blossoms that grows more than 30 feet high. The shafts are so saturated with resin that shepherds ignite them to light their way.

Get a Grip: Zulu mothers wear their hair in such a manner that their children can cling to it for security when riding piggyback.

Amazon.pod: Giant pods that protect the buds on palm trees are used by people of the Brazilian jungle as bathtubs.

Barely Believable: Donald Duck comic books were once banned in Finland because Donald didn't wear pants.

Pup Power: Nanay children in Siberia travel to and from their distant school on skis pulled by dogs.

Would You Believe?

In ancient Rome, a bad haircut was thought to . . .

a. lead to baldness.
b. encourage violence.
c. turn one's hair gray.
d. cause storms.

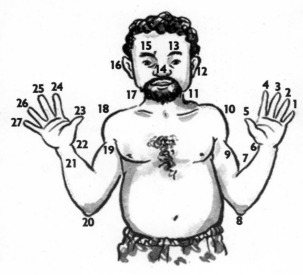

Body Count:

Instead of counting by tens as Westerners do, the people of the Min tribe in Papua New Guinea count by 27s—not only on their fingers, but on various other body parts. They begin counting on the little finger of their left hand.

Then, when they run out of fingers, they count the left wrist, forearm, elbow, biceps, shoulder, side of the neck, ear, and eye—that's 13. The bridge of the nose makes 14. Then they count the right eye, ear, side of the neck, shoulder, biceps, elbow, forearm, wrist, and five right fingers to reach a total of 27.

Just Spit It Out:

It's considered good manners in Kenya for Masai warriors to spit at each other when they meet.

High on Themselves: In
Belgium, a group of men called Les Echassiers perform combat moves, kicking and hopping while on stilts. The tradition dates back to the 15th century.

Would You Believe?

Men in Romania once had to obtain a government permit to . . .

a. walk barefoot.
b. carry an umbrella.
c. shave their beards.
d. grow a beard.

Leaf Luge: Instead of using sleds, the Iraku children of Africa slide down mountainsides on large cactus leaves.

Knee-On Lights: In
Israel's Negev Desert, camels are required to wear reflectors on their knees at night.

Earth Tones:

In Caryville, Florida, there is an annual International Worm Fiddling contest in which contestants play music to draw earthworms out of the soil.

Crop Raising:

To protect their vegetables from ants and animals, indigenous people in the Orinoco forests of South America plant their crops in boats set on frames high above the ground.

Sea Scrawlers: Sea urchin spines, which can reach six inches long, are used as pencils by schoolchildren on the Pacific island of Rarotonga.

Totem Calls: In the South Pacific islands of Vanuatu, trees are carved and hollowed out to make huge, resonant drums that are used for interisland communication.

On Pins and Needles: A popular amusement among the rural population of Bohemia in the Czech Republic is an annual pin-sticking contest to determine the best human pincushion. In 1928, the king of a Gypsy tribe won the contest by enduring 3,200 needles in his arm for a period of 31 hours. His record has never been broken.

Would You Believe?

The Yoruba people of Africa must give a gift to every woman they pass who is . . .

a. engaged.
b. holding twins.
c. in mourning.
d. a newlywed.

Fee, Fi, Fo, Fum:

A type of bean pod found in Myanmar grows to a height of four feet and is so sturdy that the Arakanese use it as a stairway to their dwellings.

Grin and Bear It:

In Romania, some people believed that a man suffering from rheumatism could recover his health by having a trained bear walk on his back for half an hour.

Sticky Situation: Once a year, the children of Ravensburg, Germany, march through the streets swinging long branches in memory of the bubonic plague in the 14th century. At the time of the plague, people were so afraid of catching the disease, they waved long sticks at one another instead of shaking hands.

Juicy Jewelry:

In New Guinea, sago-maggots are worn as jewelry but can also serve as a snack for hungry travelers.

Trick or Treat: In the United States, a company makes InsectNside— amber-colored candies that are filled with real bugs. *Bon appétit!*

A Hot Time: Medieval monks created primitive alarm clocks by placing a lit candle between their toes. When the flame singed their skin, they knew it was time to rise and shine.

Would You Believe?

It was once against the law in Indiana to kiss someone if you had . . .

a. a beard.
b. pierced ears.
c. influenza.
d. poison ivy.

Royal Shock Absorbers: In Germany during the 19th century, every prince had a *purgelknaben,* a boy who was raised with the young prince and spanked whenever the prince misbehaved.

Snakes in the Grass: Female snake-worshipers of Dahomey, Africa, are obliged to pick up every snake they encounter and transport it to the nearest temple— wearing it like a necklace!

Would You Believe?

The polite way to greet someone in Tibet is to . . .

a. kick stones out of his or her path.
b. hand him or her a piece of fresh fruit.
c. bow and stick out your tongue three times.
d. yodel.

Brain Buster

Check out the following four fantastic human abilities and figure out which one is completely made up.

a. In 1935, El Gran Lazaro of Havana, Cuba, put a needle in his eye socket and pulled it out of his mouth!
Believe It!   Not!

b. Twelve-year-old Matthew Jenkins of Omaha, Nebraska, can catch and eat flies with his tongue. He says they taste like crunchy raisins.
Believe It!   Not!

c. It took Jedediah Buxton one month to figure out that someone could fit 586,040,972,673,024,000 human hairs into one cubic mile.
Believe It!   Not!

d. Jim Purol can stuff 151 drinking straws into his mouth.
Believe It!   Not!

BONUS QUESTION

When the people in Yamanakako, Japan, get stressed out, they have a special way of relieving tension. What do they do?

a. They rent megaphones and scream at the top of their lungs until they shatter all the glass in their immediate vicinity.

b. They rent "relief rooms" where they can take their frustrations out by smashing reproductions of antiques.

c. They put on special foam rubber suits and rent "rubber rooms" where they can fling themselves at the walls and bounce off without getting injured.

CHAPTER 5 Out of the Odd-inary

Everyone has his or her own natural abilities and strengths. It's just that some seem more unnatural than others.

Sketchy Stunt: In 1934, Tom Breen of New York used both his hands and his feet to simultaneously write in four languages as well as draw cartoons.

Would You Believe?

What United States president could simultaneously write in Latin with one hand and in Greek with the other?

a. James A. Garfield.
b. Dwight D. Eisenhower.
c. Richard M. Nixon.
d. Franklin D. Roosevelt.

Suspension of Disbelief: Members of the Texas-based Traumatic Stress Discipline Club are hooked on having themselves hoisted into the air by ropes, cables, and pulleys that are attached to hooks pierced through their skin.

Pressing Engagement: Using pain-deadening meditation, Tim Cridland can lie on a bed of nails and allow a 3,000-pound vehicle to drive over him.

Human Pincushion: A featured performer at the Dallas, Texas, Odditorium in 1937, A. Bryant would stick up to a hundred pins and needles into his body at one time.

Head Trip: In 1931, entertainer Alexandre Patty bounced up and down a flight of stairs on his head.

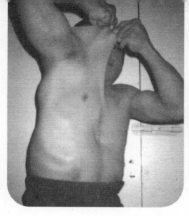

Thin Skin: Las Vegas contortionist and performer Thomas Martin Peres, also known as "Mr. Stretch," loves to shock people by pulling the skin of his neck up over his nose like a turtleneck sweater.

Would You Believe?

New members are admitted to the Bird Men, a secret society of acrobatic dancers in Guinea, Africa, only if they can . . .

a. stand on their head.
b. walk on their hands.
c. hop on one hand.
d. swivel their head 180 degrees.

Tongue Depressor: In 1938, Leona Young of Norwich, New York, astounded audiences with her ability to withstand the heat of a plumber's blowtorch on her tongue—earning her the nickname the "Devil's Daughter."

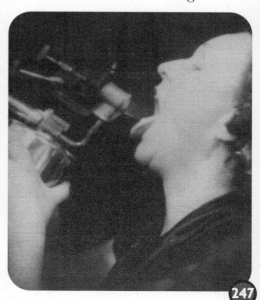

The Write Stuff:

In 1942, Lena Deeter of Conway, Arkansas, amazed audiences by showing them how she could simultaneously write with both hands in different directions.

Birdcalls: Elie

Gourbeyre of Nouara, France, could lure any bird to her shoulder merely by crooking her finger. This strange talent lasted only from the time she was six until she was 12 years old.

Painless in Pittsburgh:

Leo Kongee of Pittsburgh, Pennsylvania, could drive nails into his nose, use thumbtacks to hold up his socks, and sew buttons onto his tongue without feeling any pain.

Would You Believe?

The Mayoruna people of Brazil insert eight-inch-long palm spines through their noses and lips and tattoo whiskers on their faces because they believe they are descended from . . .

a. mountain lions.
b. tigers.
c. rats.
d. panthers.

By the Skin of Her Teeth: In 1934, aerialist Tiny Kline glided across Times Square 100 feet off the ground—while hanging by her mouth! She was fitted with a special mouthpiece attached to a pulley for the stunt.

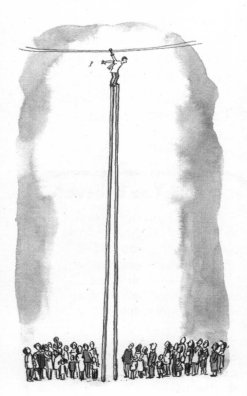

Stiff Competition: Not everyone is tall, but there are other ways to reach new heights. Meet the Wolf family. For ten years, Edward Wolf held the record for walking on the tallest pair of stilts ever—40 feet 9.5 inches to be exact. Then in 1998, his son Travis broke that record by walking on stilts that were 40 feet 10.25 inches high. Travis hopes he'll keep his title a long time, but the odds are getting smaller since siblings Ashley, Tony, and Jordan are well on their way to catching up with him.

Rubber Face:

J. T. Saylors of Memphis, Tennessee, was able to "swallow" his nose.

On Bended Knee:

In the 1930s, F. Velez Campos of Puerto Rico had his own unique way of kneeling down.

Would You Believe?

Vaudeville contortionist King Brawn could fit his entire body . . .

a. into a balloon.
b. through a tennis racket.
c. through a basketball hoop.
d. into a clothes dryer.

Human Owl:

Martin Joe Laurello drew large crowds to Ripley's Odditoriums throughout the 1930s. His ability to swivel his head 180 degrees never failed to amaze audiences.

All Bottled Up: Hugo Zamarate

of Argentina is five feet nine inches tall, but he can fold his body to fit into a bottle that's only 26 inches high and 18 inches wide.

Head Case: In the 1930s, Lorraine Chevalier of

Philadelphia, Pennsylvania, could sit on her own head. The famous Chevalier family of acrobats claimed that only one person was born into their family every 200 years who was capable of attaining this position.

Thick Skin:

H. H. Getty of Edmonton, Alberta, Canada, discovered that a lit match held to his skin caused neither pain nor blistering. Though Getty visited several prominent physicians, no explanation was ever found.

It's the Buzz!

In ancient Greece, women wore live cicadas leashed to golden thread as ornaments for their hair.

So Bee-Coming:

When Fred Wilcutt of Falkville, Alabama, captured a queen bee and placed it under his chin, the colony of bees arranged itself around his jaw and neck like a beard.

Nosing Around:

In 1934, Joe Horowitz of Los Angeles, California, known as "The Man with the Iron Nose," balanced an 18-pound sword on the tip of his nose. He could perform the same feat with a lighted torch.

Would You Believe?

In 1919, British circus performer Edith Clifford swallowed a . . .

a. 23-inch bayonet that was fired from a cannon.
b. lightbulb.
c. lit torch.
d. double-edged sword.

Handy Trick: In 1940, Blanche Lowe, a waitress at Clayton's Café in Tyler, Texas, could carry 23 coffee cups in one hand.

Would You Believe?

Jim Chicon can inhale milk through one of his nostrils and spray it out from . . .

a. one of his ears.
b. his mouth.
c. his other nostril.
d. one of his eyes.

The Unvarnished Truth: In the 1940s, Joe Jirgles of Grand Rapids, Michigan, could hold a one-gallon can of varnish between his shoulder blades. He could also use his shoulder blades to attach himself to a fence so firmly that he could hang in place.

Quick Change Artist:
In 1933, Max Calvin of
Brooklyn, New York,
never had to fish for
change. He could hold
25 quarters in his ear.

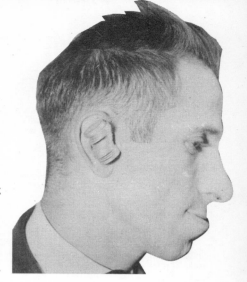

**Popping Out for a
Moment:** Avelino Perez
Matos of Cuba could
amaze people by
popping his eyeballs in
and out of their sockets.

Sight for Sore Eyes: In 1933, Odditorium performer
Harry McGregor used his eyelids to pull a wagon
carrying his wife.

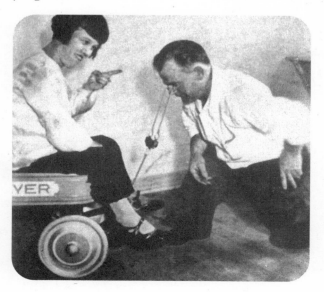

Tale End:

C. J. Anderson wrote all his correspondence upside down and backward.

Would You Believe?

In the 1890s, vaudeville performer William Leroy could extract large spikes from a two-inch plank using only . . .

a. his teeth.
b. his fingers.
c. his toes.
d. tweezers.

You know what you have to do—find the fiction!

a. In November 1989, Polly Ketron arranged and attended her own funeral. She celebrated her 76th birthday two days later.
Believe It!   Not!

b. Erik Soderberg of Pittsburgh, Pennsylvania, had the lyrics of the Pokémon theme song tattooed on the inside of his lower lip.
Believe It!   Not!

c. Sy Bondy of Miami, Florida, collects a penny from every person he meets. Within one two-month period, he collected five million pennies or $50,000 in cash!
Believe It!   Not!

d. For a period of 23 years, Arthur E. Gehrke of Watertown, Wisconsin, hibernated by staying in bed each winter from Thanksgiving until Easter.
Believe It!   Not!

BONUS QUESTION

According to an article published by the *Toronto Star* in 1998, what was so unusual about the theft of a cement frog from the garden of John and Gertrude Knight in Swansea, Massachusetts?

a. This garden decoration was valued at over $200,000,000!

b. The "frog-nappers" sent anonymous cards and letters to the owners from all over the world detailing the frog's exploits, then returned the garden decoration months later.

c. The teenagers who "borrowed" the Knights' cement frog made a digital mini-movie in which the frog skateboarded off the roof of the Knights' house, did a double back flip, and landed right back in the garden—unassisted. The Knights would never have known except that one of the filmmakers sent the video to the couple from an e-mail address that included his own last name.

POP QUIZ

It's not over yet. How much do you remember about the oddest of the odd? It's time to find out. Circle your answers and give yourself five points for each question you answer correctly.

1. You wouldn't believe the things people eat. Or would you? Which of these crazy cuisine facts is *not* true?
a. King Henry III of France dined on partridges coated with gold and poultry soaked in perfume.
b. In the British countryside, shepherds drink the milk and blood of sheep for good luck—but they never eat the meat!
c. In New Guinea, people snack on sago maggots. YUM!

2. Which of the following oddities is so *not* true?
a. Pierre Messie of France was born with an extra nostril.
b. Francesco Lentini of Sicily was born with three legs.
c. Liu Ch'ung of China was born with two pupils in each eye.

3. Susan E. Weiss, of West Hempstead, New York, was born with a full set of teeth in her mouth!

Believe It!   **Not!**

4. Which of the following was considered beautiful by fashionable women in Japan during the Middle Ages?
a. Elongated necks.
b. Stretched earlobes.
c. Blackened teeth.

5. Which of the following sensational surgeries has *not* actually been performed?

a. Performance artist Auralest had a third ear attached.

b. Alfred Hitchcock had his navel removed.

c. The "Bride of Wildenstein" had surgery to make her look like a cat.

6. At the age of two, baby Murasaki Shikibu could . . .

a. repeat 1,000 lines of poetry she had heard only once.

b. jump rope for five hours straight.

c. determine the pH level of a substance just by looking at it.

7. People are strange, and then they get stranger. Michel Lotito mystifies friends and strangers by . . .

a. freezing and thawing his body up to 30 times a day.

b. chewing and swallowing razor blades, bolts, glasses, and bicycles.

c. designing sportswear made out of soybeans and tofu.

8. Which one of the following feats is *so* amazingly false?

a. German circus performer Miss Heliot carried a 660-pound lion on her shoulders.

b. Every year, Balanta women in Guinea Bissau, Africa, perform a dance while balancing a basket holding their husband or sweetheart on their head.

c. Susan Dae of Tampa, Florida, subdued a runaway tiger with her bare hands and returned it to the nearby zoo without sustaining any injuries.

9. What's so special about Professor Bill Steed?

a. He studies frog psychology at Croaker College and uses hypnosis to train frogs to perform amazing feats like lifting barbells.

b. He studies the saliva of Komodo dragons in an attempt to find an antidote for biological warfare. Why? These reptiles are immune to each other's poison, and the secret to this amazing property could save lives.

c. He trains roaches to perform in a minicircus. With cues from a high-pitched whistle, he can make them walk on a tightrope, swing on the trapeze, and jump through flaming hoops.

10. Hard to believe, but only one of the following rare royal behaviors is *not* true. Can you figure out which one?

a. The eighth Earl of Bridgewater dressed his dogs in fine clothing and let them eat dinner at his table every day.

b. Whenever his favorite dog had puppies, King Henry III of France carried the litter in a basket slung from his neck for days.

c. Queen Isabella of Spain used her dog to judge the trustworthiness of visitors to the court. If the dog growled, the visitor was immediately banished to the New World.

11. Which of the following is completely false?
a. Elementary school kids in Patzcuaro, Mexico, trained an elephant to pick up a watering can, wet down the walls of their school, then wipe them down with a large brush.
b. Schoolchildren on the Pacific Island of Rarotonga use the spines of sea urchins as pencils. Each spine is about six inches long.
c. Nanay children in Siberia travel to and from their distant school on skis pulled by dogs.

12. Masai warriors in Kenya spit at each other when they meet—and it's considered good manners!
                    Believe It!   **Not!**

13. Leo Kongee of Pittsburgh felt no pain—he drove nails into his nose, used thumbtacks to hold up his socks, and sewed buttons onto his tongue.
                    Believe It!   **Not!**

14. Super Strong. Super Strange. Performer Harry McGregor was extraordinary because he could pull which of the following?
a. A pick-up truck filled with his entire high school marching band—a combined weight of 12,720 pounds!
b. His wife in a wagon using only his eyelids.
c. A parade float carrying the entire U.S. Olympic wrestling team, using only one arm.

15. Fourteen-year-old Arnold Ariello can sneeze with his eyes open. If his eyes pop out he just pushes them right back in.
                    Believe It!   **Not!**

Answer Key

Chapter 1

Would You Believe?

Page 189:   **b.** nose.
Page 190:   **c.** only half a body.
Page 193:   **a.** beards.
Page 195:   **c.** a hairy 18-inch-long mane.
Page 197:   **c.** seven feet eight inches.
Page 199:   **d.** six fingers on each hand.
Page 200:   **a.** support the three-foot-tall hairstyles of the day.
Brain Buster: c. is false.
Bonus Question: b.

Chapter 2

Would You Believe?

Page 203:   **c.** was accepted at the University of Pennsylvania.
Page 204:   **a.** at the age of four.
Page 207:   **d.** the names of all 4,500 officers in the British Navy and the ship to which each was assigned.
Page 209:   **b.** in his teeth.
Page 211:   **c.** hair.
Page 213:   **d.** gave blood.
Page 215:   **a.** coconut.
Page 216:   **d.** had a car suspended on wires swung into his chest like a pendulum.
Brain Buster: c. is false.
Bonus Question: b.

Chapter 3

Would You Believe?

Page 219: **d.** with his feet in ice water.

Page 221: **c.** cats.

Page 223: **b.** human hair.

Page 225: **d.** hedgehog livers.

Page 226: **b.** he was afraid of water.

Page 229: **c.** with a lobster on a leash.

Page 230: **c.** lay in an open coffin.

Brain Buster: a. is false.

Bonus Question: c.

Chapter 4

Would You Believe?

Page 233: **b.** wear his wife's clothing.

Page 234: **d.** cause storms.

Page 236: **d.** grow a beard.

Page 238: **b.** holding twins.

Page 241: **a.** a beard.

Page 242: **c.** bow and stick out your tongue three times.

Brain Buster: b. is false.

Bonus Question: b.

Chapter 5

Would You Believe?

Page 245: **a.** James A. Garfield.

Page 247: **d.** swivel their head 180 degrees.

Page 248: **c.** rats.

Page 250: **b.** through a tennis racket.

Page 253: **a.** 23-inch bayonet that was fired from a cannon.

Page 254: **d.** one of his eyes.

Page 256: **a.** his teeth.

Brain Buster: b. is false.

Bonus Question: b.

Pop Quiz

1.   **b.**
2.   **a.**
3.   **Not!**
4.   **c.**
5.   **a.**
6.   **a.**
7.   **b.**
8.   **c.**
9.   **a.**
10.   **c.**
11.   **a.**
12.   **Believe It!**
13.   **Believe It!**
14.   **b.**
15.   **Not!**

What's Your Ripley's Rank?

Ripley's Scorecard

Congrats! You've busted your brain over some of the oddest human behavior in the world and proven your ability to tell fact from fiction. Now it's time to rate your Ripley's knowledge. Are you are an Extreme Oddball or *So* Ordinary? Check out the answers in the answer key and use this page to keep track of how many trivia questions you've answered correctly. Then add 'em up and find out how you rate.

Here's the scoring breakdown—give yourself:

★ **10 points** for every **Would You Believe?** you answered correctly;

★ **20 points** for every fiction you spotted in the **Ripley's Brain Busters**;

★ **10** for every **Bonus Question** you answered right;

★ and **5** for every **Pop Quiz** question you answered correctly.

Here's a tally sheet:

Number of **Would You Believe?** _____ x 5 = _____
questions answered correctly:

Number of **Ripley's Brain Buster** _____ x 10 = _____
questions answered correctly:

Number of **Bonus Questions** _____ x 5 = _____
answered correctly:

Chapter Total: _____

Write your totals for each chapter and the Pop Quiz section in the spaces below. Then add them up to get your FINAL SCORE. Your FINAL SCORE decides how you rate:

Chapter 1 Total: _____

Chapter 2 Total: _____

Chapter 3 Total _____

Chapter 4 Total: _____

Chapter 5 Total: _____

Pop Quiz Total: _____

FINAL SCORE: _____

525–301
Extreme Oddball

You can't be fooled. You are fully aware of how strange the truth is and how odd human behavior can be. Your skill for spotting tall tales is beyond belief. Your brain never busts—even on the toughest Brain Busters. You amaze your friends and awe your family with your knowledge of the unusual, the unbelievable, and the just plain wacky. Perhaps your superskills will land you in the Ripley's files—you're already unbelievably amazing! Believe It!

300–201
Oddly Talented

Your talent for the twisted is top-notch, and you're not afraid who knows it. Why obsess over the mundane when you can focus on the fantastic? A man who lifts weights with his ear, a woman who lifts lions—bring it on! Sometimes you get stuck on a superhard Brain Buster, but let's face it, there's always room for improvement. Overall, your ability to tell fact from fiction is out of the ordinary. Trust your instincts and go, go, go!

200–101
Odd One Out

Your radar for the ridiculous is more than a little off-kilter—but you're not giving up anytime soon. You've got the basics of finding the fiction among the facts down, but you need practice on the more challenging stuff. Stories about people sticking needles in their eyes or surgically removing their belly buttons are just too bizarre for your taste. That works. Just remember, sometimes the truth is truly more bizarre than fiction.

100–0
So Ordinary

The odds are against you in this game. Tales that would freak out or amaze your friends are simply humdrum and ho-hum in your world. Maybe your everyday life is wackier than the weirdest Ripley's oddity or perhaps you have better things to do with your time. Whatever the case, separating the true from the false is just not your thing. That's okay. But consider yourself warned—people are strange, and the truth is even stranger!

Photo Credits

Ripley Entertainment Inc. and the editors of this book wish to thank the following photographers, agents, and other individuals for permission to use and reprint the following photographs in this book. Any photographs included in this book that are not acknowledged below are property of the Ripley Archives. Great effort has been made to obtain permission from the owners of all materials included in this book. Any errors that may have been made are unintentional and will gladly be corrected in future printings if notice is sent to Ripley Entertainment Inc., 5728 Major Boulevard, Orlando, Florida 32819.

198 Padaung Girl/CORBIS

205 Wolfgang Amadeus Mozart/Library of Congress, Prints and Photographs Division, Detroit Publishing Company Collection

206 Paul Erdös/by George Csicsery from his documentary film *N Is a Number: A Portrait of Paul Erdös* (1993)

215 Julia Butterfly Hill/Shaun Walker/ ottermedia.com

216 Kris Holm/Ryan Leach

221 Alfred Hitchcock/Photo Raymond Voinquel © Ministère de la Culture, France

222 Gene Pool/Gary Sutton

228 J. Pierpont Morgan/Bettmann/CORBIS

235 Masai Warriors/Steven Drummond

238 Sea Urchin/CORBIS

241 InsectNside/Courtest of HotLix

World's
Weirdest
Critters

Contents

Introduction

Welcome to the weird and wonderful world of *Ripley's Believe It or Not!* Robert Ripley was the first millionaire cartoonist in history. A real-life "Indiana Jones," he traveled all over the world, tracking down amazing facts, oddities, and curiosities.

As a lifelong animal-lover, Ripley found the creatures he encountered in his travels especially appealing: the hairy frog from central Africa; the blood-sucking vampire bat from South America; and the duck-billed, web-footed platypus that would surely take first place in a contest for world's weirdest critter.

Ripley featured many of the animals he saw in the cartoons he drew for newspapers, and he started a file of fascinating animal facts that continues to grow to this day. As long as an animal is weird enough, it is guaranteed a place of honor in the files of Ripley's Believe It or Not!

In addition to the fabulous, the wild, and the exotic, Ripley was fascinated by the naturally occurring oddities in more common animals. He encountered such marvels as a dog with two noses, a mouse with two tails, a frog with six legs, and even a snake, a turtle, and a calf that each had the unfortunate distinction of being born with two heads.

World's Weirdest Critters is a dynamic collection of amazing animal facts straight from the archives of Ripley's Believe It or Not! Its pages are chock-full of wacky characters, like the bird that plucks hair from the heads of passersby to make a cozy nest, the dog that yodels instead of barking, the snake that can spray poisonous venom instead of biting, and the sea cucumber that regurgitates its insides when it's frightened.

You'll find all these incredible creatures and tons more in the pages of *World's Weirdest Critters*. While you're at it, you'll get a chance to test your critter smarts by answering the Who Am I? questions and completing the Ripley Brain Busters in each chapter. Then take the special Pop Quiz at the end of the book and use the scorecard to find out your Ripley's Rank. So get ready to meet some of the weirdest critters on the face of the earth. Their antics will amaze you.

Believe It!

CHAPTER 1

Mirror, Mirror on the Wall . . .

Who is the strangest of us all?

Some animals have such long tongues . . . they can use them to clean their ears . . .

Once called "camelopards" (a combination of the words *camel* and *leopard*), **giraffes** use their long prehensile (used-for-grabbing) tongues to pull leaves from trees. The average giraffe spends 16 to 20 hours a day collecting food, and eats up to 140 pounds of leaves.

. . . or to catch 30,000 ants in one day.

It's lucky that the **anteater** has such a long, sticky tongue because it doesn't have any teeth. The anteater's tongue can extend as far as two feet. Besides being sticky, it's covered with tiny spines that keep the ants from getting away.

Some animals have eyes as big as pizza pies . . .

Giant squid have the largest eyes of any animal. One reason their eyes are so big is that they are huge animals. A giant squid can weigh as much as 1,980 pounds! Scientists don't know for sure where giant squid live, but they suspect the squid live between 660 and 2,300 feet below the ocean's surface. And that's another reason for the squid to have such large eyes. They probably help the squid to use what little light there is at that depth to see.

Some have not two eyes, but three . . .

The **tuatara** has an extra eye on the top of its head. Scientists think that this eye is used as a light sensor to help the tuatara keep track of its time in the sun. It may also help with directions by keeping track of the sun's position in the sky.

Who Am I?

Like most animals, I have two eyes. It's the way I close my eyelids that's different. My eyes close from the bottom up.

Am I . . .

a. a snake?
b. a rabbit?
c. a gopher?
d. a turtle?

Some animals have sweat that looks like blood . . .

but it's really a kind of skin conditioner.

The **hippopotamus** needs this oily secretion because it spends much of the day lying in water. Without it, the hippo's skin would probably get all wrinkly like a prune. Scientists think that this oily substance also protects hippos from sunburn, and it may guard against infections as well.

Other animals don't perspire at all . . .

Because neither **tigers** nor **wolves** sweat, they need another means of cooling their body. So, just like dogs, they pant. The air rushing into the animal's mouth contacts the thin, wet skin inside and helps keep its temperature down.

Some frogs have hair . . .

Certain **frogs** in the Democratic Republic of the Congo, a country in central Africa, look like they have hair. Their hips and thighs are covered with this hair, which can be as much as an inch long.

Some cats are bald . . .

The **sphynx,** a breed of hairless cat, has been recognized by the Cat Fanciers' Association since 1998. The first hairless cats were born as a result of natural genetic mutations. Then in the 1960s, people started to breed sphynx cats.

Who Am I?

I am a type of domestic cat that has no tail.

Am I . . .

a. a Manx?
b. a sphynx?
c. a Persian?
d. a Siamese?

Some birds have stubs for wings . . .

Because its wings are so small, the **kiwi** cannot fly. Named for its call, the kiwi is the national bird of New Zealand.

Some birds can't fly, but know how to bark . . .

The barking **cagou** is native to New Caledonia, an island in the western South Pacific that is about the size of New Jersey. The bird lives in the mountains and coastal rain forests. Once on the endangered list, the cagou is making a comeback because of a captive breeding program.

And some dogs don't bark—they yodel.

The **basenji**'s yodel ranges from a soft crow to a piercing scream. Originally from central Africa, the basenji is thought to be one of the oldest breeds of dog. No one is really sure why these dogs yodel. Some people think they do it when they are happy. Why do basenjis sound different from other breeds of dog? Perhaps it's because their voice box is in a different place.

Some body parts are good for resting . . .

Who Am I?

I use my tail as an umbrella, a sunshade, and a blanket.

Am I . . .

a. a peacock?
b. a squirrel?
c. a ferret?
d. a beaver?

The **Abyssinian ground hornbill**, a turkey-sized bird found in the dry savannas of parts of Africa, takes a rest by leaning on its beak. These birds can fly, but they prefer to walk, and they catch most of their food on the ground. Their diet includes lizards, tortoises, and small birds as well as some fruits and seeds.

And some are good for moving on ice . . .

The **walrus** can use its long tusks to pull itself out of the water and up onto the Arctic ice. Both male and female walruses have tusks. The tusks don't appear until the animal is about a year old, and they continue to grow for 15 years. The tusks of the male walrus grow longer than those of the female. They can be as long as 39 inches!

Some creatures have more parts than they need . . .

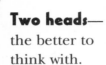

Two heads—
the better to
think with.

Who Am I?

You might say that
I have at least four
lives, since I have
four hearts to keep
me going.

Am I . . .

a. a centipede?
b. a starfish?
c. an earthworm?
d. a horseshoe
crab?

Two tails— the better to scare with.

Two noses—the better to smell with.

Six legs—the better to leap with.

289

While some are missing a few . . .

Wins more attention this way . . .
This strange-looking chicken was born without a beak.

Gets by with a little help from its friends . . .
Missing its front legs when it was born, this pony needed some support to get around.

Short on legs, long on attitude . . .
Although it had no hips or hind legs, this puppy could run almost as fast as a normal four-legged pup.

Others have parts that keep on growing.

Crocodiles

continue to grow replacement teeth for as long as they live. They can grow as many as 3,000 teeth over the course of their lives. That's a lot to smile about!

Before winter, the **ruffed grouse** grows special snowshoes. A fringe on each toe prevents it from sinking into the snow. These fringes are probably one of the reasons that grouse thrive during severe winters.

Found throughout North America, grouse prefer the aspen forests around the Great Lakes.

Who Am I?

One of my eyes has 13,000 lenses and 13,000 nerve rods. Yet if I should happen to lose one, I don't have to worry. I'll simply grow a new one.

Am I . . .

a. a human?
b. an ant?
c. a lobster?
d. a honeybee?

And some animals look all mixed up . . .

The **okapi** has striped legs like a zebra, a head like a giraffe, a neck like a horse, a body like an antelope, a tail like an ox, and a blue-black tongue that measures two feet long. Okapis, which are relatives of the giraffe, live in the rain forests of central Africa.

The **aardvark** has the body of a giant, hump-backed rat with the head of an anteater, the snout of a pig, the ears of a bear, the thick, powerful tail of a kangaroo, the claws of a tiger, and a flat tongue that's one and a half feet long!

Who Am I?

I produce venom like a snake. I'm a mammal, but I lay eggs like a bird. I have the bill and feet of a duck, and the tail of a beaver.

Am I . . .

a. an armadillo?
b. an aardvark?
c. a Tasmanian devil?
d. a platypus?

Ripley's Believe It or Not! Brain Buster

Ready to test your knowledge of the mind-blowingly bizarre, the super-strange, and the amazingly unbelievable?

The Ripley files are packed with info that's too out-there to believe. Each shocking oddity proves that truth is stranger than fiction. But it takes a keen eye, a sharp mind, and good instincts to spot the difference. Are you up for the challenge?

Each Ripley's Brain Buster contains a group of four unbelievable oddities. In each group of oddities only **ONE** is **FALSE**. Read each extraordinary entry and circle whether you **Believe It!** or **Not!** And if you think you can handle it, take on the bonus question in each section. Then, flip to the end of the book where you'll find a place to keep track of your score and rate your skills.

Which is stranger, fact or fiction? Can you tell? Check out this Ripley's Brain Buster. Remember, only one entry is false.

a. A mouse has more bones in its body than a human.

Believe It!   **Not!**

b. A single beaver can chomp down a tree five inches in diameter in only three minutes.

Believe It!   **Not!**

c. In addition to the ability to turn its head 180 degrees, an owl can fly upside down and backward.

Believe It!   Not!

d. A headless chicken laid an egg in Elizabethtown, Kentucky.

Believe It!   Not!

• •

BONUS QUESTION

Why was a Labrador retriever named Endel declared Dog of the Millennium by a dog food company?

a. Endel can pick up items from supermarket shelves, withdraw money from the ATM, and load and unload the washer and dryer. After he was injured during the Gulf War, Endel's owner worked out a special sign language with the dog. All he has to do is tap the top of his head, touch his cheek, or rub his hands together, and Endel knows to fetch his hat, razor, or gloves.

b. Endel uses his heightened canine senses to detect earthquakes before they strike. Before a quake hit Seattle, Washington, in 2001, Endel refused to eat. When the quake struck, he managed to get his owner to safety before their entire house collapsed.

c. Endel guided every ship in and out of Hatteras Inlet, off the coast of North Carolina, from 1910 to 1912, by running up and down the shore with a large beacon in his mouth. He never lost a single vessel.

CHAPTER 2

What's for Dinner?

Some critters don't have to eat very often . . .

The **pheasant** can live for an entire month without eating. Ring-necked pheasants are found in the wild in much of the northern United States. These birds were brought to America from China in 1881.

Others eat as often as they can . . .

Some people believe that the **cormorant** eats twice its weight in fish every day, but recent studies show that it only eats about 25 percent of its body weight. That means a four-pound bird eats about a pound of fish a day. In many parts of the world, cormorants in captivity catch fish for the people who raise them. The birds are fitted with a special neck strap that prevents them from swallowing.

The **little brown bat** can eat more than 3,000 insects, including mosquitoes, in one night. Some hungry bats even consume 1,200 insects in one hour. Bats use echolocation, a kind of sonar, to find their prey.

295

Some critters are picky eaters . . .

The **Siberian brown bear** eats only fish heads.

The **Siberian white-breasted bear** throws away the fish heads. It only eats the bodies.

Who Am I?

When I get very hungry, I go hunting for sheep.

Am I a type of . . .

a. parrot?
b. zebra?
c. hippopotamus?
d. elephant?

Others are not picky at all . . .

The **kiwi** eats its weight in worms. Unlike most birds, the kiwi's nostrils are at the end of its long, thin bill, which the bird uses to search the ground for its wriggly breakfast, lunch, and dinner.

Some creatures have a mighty thirst . . .

The **vampire bat**, a small bat of South America and Mexico, drinks more than its own weight in blood every night.

The **hummingbird** drinks the nectar of 1,000 flowers each day. It needs to drink a lot because it uses up so much energy flying around. This bird can flap its wings 55 to 75 beats per second. If trapped indoors, a hummingbird can starve to death within one hour.

Other creatures don't drink much at all . . .

Except in times of drought, the **koala** gets all its fluids from the eucalyptus leaves it eats. Because their diet of leaves is so low in nutritional value, koalas sleep about 16 hours a day. Sometimes called a koala bear, this critter is not a bear at all, but a marsupial.

Some animals take teeny, tiny bites . . .

Even though its mouth is so large a human adult male can stand inside it, the **blue whale** doesn't swallow anything bigger than a shrimp. Instead of teeth, this whale has baleen, a series of plates that hang down from the upper jaw and act as strainers. To collect food, blue whales strain gallons and gallons of seawater every day. Their main food source is krill, which are tiny shrimp-like creatures. Because the blue whale is the world's largest mammal, measuring between 75 and 100 feet long and weighing as many as 110 tons, it may eat as much as four tons of krill a day.

Some work hard for every bite . . .

The **silvery gull** breaks the shells of snails and mussels by dropping them from great heights. The gull will drop a single shell as many times as it takes to shatter.

Who Am I?

I have a very big appetite. In fact, I often swallow fish that are larger than I am. It's a good thing that my stomach and gullet are so stretchable.

Am I . . .

a. a shark?
b. a blowfish?
c. a sea bass?
d. a pelican eel?

The **peregrine falcon** dives at its prey at speeds of over 200 miles an hour. Then it zooms under its victim, turns on its back, and catches the wounded prey in its claws.

Some critters swallow things whole . . .

The **secretary bird** can swallow a hen's egg without breaking the shell. In the wild, this bird typically eats snakes, lizards, tortoises, mice, smaller birds, and sometimes grasshoppers. It often swallows small prey whole and alive. This bird, which stands between three and four feet high and rarely flies, lives and hunts on the plains and grasslands of Africa. On farms, tame secretary birds keep the fields free of snakes.

A **sea snake** swallows the fish it eats whole. Because of its hinged jaw, this snake can open its mouth wide enough to swallow a fish more than twice the diameter of its own neck. Sea snakes measure three to five feet long and are found in the Indian and Pacific Oceans. Like its relative, the cobra, the sea snake's venom is poisonous to people as well as to its prey.

Who Am I?

I leave the water and climb into the branches of high trees to search for food.

Am I a type of . . .

a. sea otter?
b. fish?
c. frog?
d. lobster?

Some eat while swimming . . .

The **elephant seal** only eats when it is underwater. Male seals fast for up to three months at a time when they come on land to molt and to breed. Females also fast, but for less time. Even the

pups go for long periods without eating. After they are weaned and their mother leaves them, the pups stay on land for eight to ten weeks and don't eat a thing the whole time. During this period, they typically lose about one-third of their body weight.

Some eat upside down . . .

A **flamingo** eats with its head held upside down. It turns its long beak so that the bottom half faces the sky, while the top half is totally underwater. Thin slits on either side of the top of its bill act as strainers. They filter out sand, mud, and insects, while keeping in the mollusks that are the flamingo's favorite food.

Some creatures fish for their food . . .

The **osprey** is the only type of hawk that dives into the water to catch its prey. To find a good fishing location, the osprey watches other birds, noting what they've caught and their flight paths. Then it dives into the water, catches the fish it prefers, and tears it apart with its talons.

The **green-backed heron** catches insects to use as bait. It drops them on the water, then swoops down to devour the fish that rise to the bait.

Who Am I?

I live in the Pacific and Indian Oceans, but when I'm hungry, I climb trees to find my favorite food— coconuts.

Am I . . .

a. a lobster?
b. a crab?
c. a snail?
d. a sea lion?

While others hunt . . .

A **polar bear** can smell and locate prey at a distance of 20 miles. It often swims far from shore to reach the seals and walrus cubs it likes to eat. Polar bears will also eat shellfish and seabirds. In a pinch, they'll even settle for seaweed. On land, the polar bear's large furry paws act like snowshoes to help it silently stalk caribou when it's in the mood for an extra-hearty dinner.

A **coyote** can hear a mouse moving under a foot of snow. Also known as the prairie wolf, the coyote is valuable to farmers because it hunts small animals such as rabbits, mice, and gophers that can damage crops. Coyotes live in most of North America. They are adaptable animals and will eat just about anything that's available, including grasshoppers and blueberries.

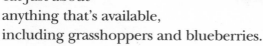

Some fish like to go fishing . . .

The female **deep-sea anglerfish** has its own built-in fishing rod. The luminous, or glowing, bit of flesh at the end of her dorsal fin serves as bait to lure her prey close enough to be snapped up. The male anglerfish attaches himself to a female, then depends on her for survival.

The **scorpion fish** also uses its dorsal fin as a lure. When raised, the fin looks like a smaller fish. Medium-size fish are attracted to the fin—and before they know it, they end up as dinner for the scorpion fish.

While some fish venture onto land . . .

During times of drought, certain types of African **catfish** leave their ponds at night to travel to bigger ponds. These fish are able to breathe air and may crawl for miles in search of a new watery home.

Who Am I?

I catch mice by drowning them in the sea.

Am I . . .

a. a porpoise?
b. a clam?
c. an oyster?
d. a seal?

304

Some creatures trap what they eat . . .

The larva, or young, of the **sand runner** catches insects by digging a trap in the sand and plugging the opening with its body.

Instead of spinning a web, the **trapdoor spider** builds a burrow with a trapdoor. The burrow is about six inches long. The trapdoor is made of dirt and is attached to the side of the burrow with silk that the spider spins. The spider camouflages the  door with leaves, sticks, and small stones. Then it hides under the door, waiting for prey to come along. When the spider hears an insect on the other side, it jumps out, grabs the bug, and pulls it into the burrow.

Others like to shoot it . . .

The **archerfish**, a freshwater fish found in Asia and Australia, uses its long snout like a gun. It shoots at insects up to three feet away with jets of water, which cause the insects to fall where the archerfish can reach them.

Some critters wait for food to find them . . .

The **moray eel** curls up and hides in a hole or under coral until prey swims by. Then it attacks with lightning speed. This eel eats damselfish, cardinal fish, octopus—and even other eels.

While some find food on trees . . .

One of the **Hanuman langur**'s favorite foods is a fruit containing strychnine, a poison deadly to humans. Although they eat a variety of things, their diet is mostly leaves. A specially designed stomach helps these monkeys break down all the fiber. In India, some people feed Hanuman langurs because they consider them sacred to the monkey god.

Who Am I?

I have a very thick-walled throat and esophagus. It's a good thing, too. Otherwise I'd get splinters from the food I like to eat.

Am I . . .

a. a giant panda?
b. a woodchuck?
c. a beaver?
d. a termite?

Bow-WOW! This doggy Brain Buster is doggone unbelievable! Are you ready to check out some bizarre canine behavior? Then take a shot at spotting which one of these Believe It! or Not! entries is false.

a. For three years a dog named Dorsey was the only mail carrier between Calico and Bismarck in California's Mojave Desert. It was a three-mile trip each way—and Dorsey always stayed on schedule.

Believe It!   Not!

b. Bonkie, an Irish setter belonging to Justin McClean of Cambridge, Massachusetts, graduated from Harvard University with a degree in The Science of Search and Rescue.

Believe It!   Not!

c. A former bomb-sniffing dog named George has been retrained to sniff out cancer in people. He has a higher success rate than X rays!

Believe It!   Not!

d. Fudge, a dog in England, swallowed a musical alarm watch. Every morning at 6:45, Fudge played a tune—like clockwork! The watch was successfully removed in an operation. You've got to shut off the alarm sometime!

Believe It!   Not!

BONUS QUESTION

What's so special about Bosco, a black Labrador retriever owned by Tim Stillman of Sunol, California?

a. Over the course of 11 years, Bosco has saved the lives of more than 30 people in this small town.

b. Bosco's been delivering newspapers and coupon circulars to the townspeople for over 16 years—without any human help.

c. Bosco was the mayor of this small community for more than eight years. He earned more votes than the two humans who ran against him for office!

Some animals' homes are hidden . . .

The male **wedge-tailed hornbill**, a large African bird, protects its mate and their eggs by hiding them in a hollow tree and plastering mud over the entrance. A tiny slit is left through which the hornbill passes food to its mate. The meals consist of food that he has swallowed and then regurgitated.

The **lion** protects its cubs in a lair hidden among rocks or in a cave. Lions usually live in rocky areas, sandy plains with thick bushes, or near streams that provide tall grasses among which to hide. The adaptable lions of the Masai Mara, an area of Kenya, actually climb trees and rest in their branches.

309

Others stand out . . .

Some **wasps** build a nest that stands out like a banner from a tree branch. The wasps make a paperlike substance by chewing on wood fibers. Then they use the mixture of fibers and saliva to build the nest. These wasps are sometimes called social wasps because, like bees, they live and work with a group of other wasps.

Some homes are delicate web sites . . .

The female **hummingbird** uses spiderwebs to help hold her tiny nest together. She also uses the fuzzy parts of cattails or dandelions to line the nest, and places lichen on the outside walls so that the nest looks like just a bump on the tree. Although this delicate structure typically measures only two inches across and two inches deep, it can take a hummingbird six to ten days to build it.

Who Am I?

The mail carriers stopped delivering the mail in my neighborhood until my babies grew up. That's because I attacked when they got too close to my nest.

Am I . . .

a. a wasp?
b. a mockingbird?
c. a bumblebee?
d. a bluejay?

Some have showers . . .

The **American dipper** often builds its globe-shaped nest in the spray of a waterfall. The mist from the waterfall keeps the outer layer of moss green. The inside, which is made of grass, stays relatively dry. Dippers use the same nests year after year. One nest has even been occupied by dippers for more than 100 years!

Some homes are quite large . . .

Built out of sticks, the nest of the **bald eagle** can weigh as much as two tons and measure nine feet across and 12 feet deep. Couples return to the same nest year after year.

While others are tiny . . .

One kind of cave-dwelling **swiftlet** doesn't use twigs to build its shelflike home. Instead, it constructs its small nest entirely from its saliva. Some people consider the nests of these small birds a delicacy and collect them to make bird's-nest soup.

Some homes come stocked with food . . .

The **solitary wasp**, which lives alone rather than in a hive, lays its eggs in a nest with paralyzed insects inside. The wasp collects the insects and stings them so they can't move. After the eggs hatch, the larvae (the young wingless wasps) eat the insects their parent has provided.

And others are equipped with air . . .

The **water spider** stocks its underwater nest with air by bringing it down in big bubbles from the surface. Tiny hairs on the spider's legs and body help it to carry the air bubbles. The spider's nest, which is made from silk that it spins, is where the creature eats.

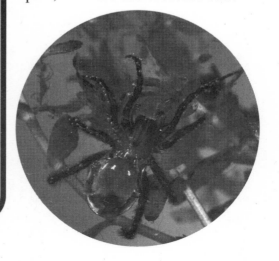

Who Am I?

I always build my nest so that one end of it points to the north and the other to the south.

Am I a type of . . .

a. ant?
b. worm?
c. lizard?
d. toad?

Some critters
make nests out of leaves . . .

The **Australian sugar glider** bites off large leaves and
carries them wrapped up in its tail. It uses the leaves to
line its nest in the hollow of a tree. A type of opossum,
the sugar glider, like a kangaroo, is a marsupial. This ten-
inch critter sails through the air by stretching the
membrane between its front and back legs and using it
like a sail.

The **tailorbird**, a type of Asian thrush, uses its beak to
poke holes in a leaf—then laces the leaf together with
grass to make a cozy nest.

Others build their nests
with stones . . .

The **lamprey eel** carries heavy
stones to construct its nest at
the bottom of the sea. The
nests of these eels can measure
as much as three feet high and
four feet around.

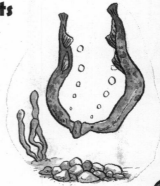

And some don't make nests at all . . .

The **puffin** lays its single egg in a burrow it digs near the coast. These seabirds of the Northern Hemisphere gather in large groups in the spring to lay their eggs. The parents take turns incubating the egg and feeding the puffling, which hatches in about six weeks.

Who Am I?

I build my mud nest in the shape of a ball. To hold it together, I plant seeds, so it soon looks like a tiny flower garden.

Am I a type of . . .

a. worm?
b. bird?
c. ant?
d. grasshopper?

Some live in high-rises . . .

Bank swallows dig burrows in the side of a cliff or a riverbank, creating bird "apartment buildings." Their tunnels can be up to three feet long. Colonies of bank swallows may contain as few as 12 pairs of birds or as many as several hundred. Bank swallows lay their eggs in the spring in many parts of North America.

Or have water views . . .

The female **pie-billed grebe** builds her nest in the form of a raft that she attaches to a reed so it won't float away.

Some work alone . . .

The male **satin bowerbird** attracts females with a nest that he has decorated with red berries, flowers, bits of colored cloth, and seashells.

Others have help . . .

The **hermit crab** lives inside its shell with a sea worm that keeps it clean. Hermit crabs don't grow their own shells, but use shells abandoned by other creatures on the ocean floor. When a hermit crab grows, it just moves into a bigger shell.

Who Am I?

Just the thought of building a nest makes me want to snooze. That's why I've perfected my imitation of a rattlesnake. One hiss and the squirrels run from home, leaving me a ready-made burrow to live in.

Am I . . .

a. a mole?
b. a prairie dog?
c. a ferret?
d. an owl?

And some work in construction crews . . .

The **agricultural ant** of Texas builds the colony's nest in an area of thick, tall grass after preparing a clearing and building a system of roads in all directions. This species of ant gets its name because it actually collects seeds, which are known as ant rice, and plants them to grow its own favorite grass.

Brain Buster

Work it! These animals get down to business in the most unbelievable ways. In each Brain Buster, one Ripley's rarity is completely made up. Can you tell which one it is?

a. Isaac is a golden retriever that can add, subtract, multiply, and divide. He even does square roots! When Isaac was a puppy, his owner Gary Wimer started spending 20 minutes a day teaching the dog to count. Now, Wimer just asks Isaac what the square root of 36 is, and Isaac barks six times!

Believe It!   **Not!**

b. A parrot named Alex has been the subject of Irene Pepperberg's research at the University of Arizona for 22 years. Alex has a vocabulary of 100 words. He can also identify 50 different objects and sort them by color, shape, and texture. Research has proven that Alex doesn't just copy what he hears but actually processes information!

Believe It!   **Not!**

c. Snowcone is a singing leopard living in New York's Bronx Zoo. Snowcone can belt out the entire melody of "The Star-Spangled Banner" as well as the theme song from *Gilligan's Island*!

Believe It!   **Not!**

d. Suti, a 6,500-pound African elephant who lived at Chicago's Lincoln Park Zoo, used his trunk to make abstract paintings.

Believe It! **Not!**

• •

BONUS QUESTION

Why does a miniature horse named Twinky need to wear little sneakers?

a. Twinky is a champion country line dancer. He's finished in first place in over 115 competitions and frequently performs at county fairs and festivals in his hometown of Elmwood, Illinois.

b. Twinky is a trained guide animal for the blind. He needs the traction to avoid slipping and sliding at the mall.

c. Twinky burned the bottom of his hooves while dragging his sleeping owner from a burning barn. The sneakers protect Twinky's sensitive hooves from rocks and debris on the ground.

Some critters help other kinds of critters . . .

The **parrot fish** balances vertically in the water while a school of smaller fish called **wrasses** use their pincerlike jaws to pick them clean of parasites.

The **Egyptian plover**, also known as the crocodile bird, picks and cleans the teeth of Nile crocodiles. These plovers eat insects and leeches, creatures that the crocodile is happy to do without. Egyptian plovers are found in several parts of Africa and in Asia.

Tickbirds, such as the **red-** or **yellow-billed oxpecker**, ride on the back of the rhinoceros. The bird eats ticks and other insects from the rhino's skin, so the rhino is less itchy. In addition to eliminating bugs, they serve as early warning systems for their four-legged friends. When predators approach, the tickbirds raise the alarm by squawking and flying away.

And some become quite attached to each other . . .

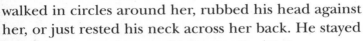

In 1986, a **moose** appeared on Larry Carrara's Vermont farm. The moose began to court one of Carrara's cows, a Hereford named Jessica. He walked in circles around her, rubbed his head against her, or just rested his neck across her back. He stayed with Jessica for 76 days.

Thousands of people came to visit this unlikely couple. After the moose left, Carrara and author Pat Wakefield wrote a book called *A Moose for Jessica*.

Who Am I?

I don't usually bond with cows, but if placed in the same pen, cattle will protect me from predators.

Am I . . .

a. a dog?
b. a sheep?
c. a cat?
d. a goose?

Other critters speak only to their own kind . . .

Honeybees communicate with a body language so subtle that only bees from the same geographical area can tell what it means. If a bee wants to tell its hive mates exactly where to find some tasty flowers, it does a kind of dance. The better the food source, the longer and more energetically the bee will dance.

Red-capped mangabeys, medium-size tree-dwelling African monkeys, communicate by using facial expressions. Mangabeys have white eyelids that are easily visible in the dim light of the forest. The white facial highlights enable these monkeys to "talk" to one another from quite a distance.

An **elephant** sends messages over long and short distances using a "secret code" of low-frequency sounds. The sounds the elephants make are quite loud, but because they are of such a low-frequency, humans cannot hear them. Other elephants can hear these low-frequency sounds from distances of more than five miles away.

Prairie dogs, a type of large, burrowing squirrel native to the western United States, identify one another by kissing. When two prairie dogs meet, they each press their teeth against the other's face. Some scientists believe that prairie dogs use touch, sounds, and body language to communicate with other prairie dogs from their own or neighboring colonies.

Who Am I?

The males of my species don't really like to fight. But if another male acts unfriendly, I act like a proud father and show him my baby. Then he forgets his threats and fusses over the baby.

Am I a type of . . .

a. manatee?
b. sea lion?
c. dolphin?
d. monkey?

The **elephant snout fish** communicates by sending out electrical signals. The electrical impulses that this freshwater fish sends out fill the water all around it. Changes in the current let the fish know what other kinds of fish are nearby.

Ermine, members of the weasel family that have long been prized for their beautiful white winter coat, mourn when one of their species dies. Ermine are native to northern areas of America and Europe.

Some critters like to be courted . . .

The female **Arctic tern** will not mate until her suitor brings her a gift. The male tern catches a fish and flies over the head of the female he is courting. If the female tern accepts his offering, she will rise up and fly with him. In the summer, Arctic terns breed in the Northern Hemisphere. Arctic terns make the longest migratory journey of any bird, flying as far away as Antarctica. Some of them travel as many as 20,000 miles a year.

And some have several mates . . .

Gorillas live in bands of six or seven, made up of one dominant male and several females and young animals. In their natural habitat in western Africa, the male gorilla breeds with the females. When a young male gorilla in the band reaches maturity, he leaves and forms his own band.

Lions live in prides of between three and 30 individuals. The females in one pride are all related to one another. When the male cubs in the pride grow up, they leave the pride and travel with other males in a group called a coalition. A coalition takes over a pride of females. After two to four years, another male coalition kicks the males out and takes over the pride.

While others mate for life . . .

If a **crane**'s mate dies, it remains a loner for the rest of its life. Cranes are tall wading birds that look a lot like herons. There are 14 different kinds of cranes, and they live all over the globe except in South America.

The **lag goose**, sometimes called the gray-lag goose, also mates for life. Most domestic geese in Europe and America are descended from the European gray-lag goose.

Some critters are equipped for a fast getaway . . .

The **flying dragon** is equipped with a pair of "wings." These are actually folds of skin stretched over its long rib bones that allow it to "fly" from tree to tree. Like flying squirrels, however, these five-inch southeast Asian lizards don't really fly, but glide. They can glide as far as 150 feet.

Who Am I?

My mate likes to sing to me. I let him know which parts of his song I like by raising my wing in approval. My mate responds by repeating those parts I liked best.

Am I . . .

a. a cowbird?
b. a mockingbird?
c. a nightingale?
d. a canary?

Or pack anti-sonar devices . . .

Bats use their special sonar, called echolocation, to track down moths and other insects. But **tiger moths** can escape capture by sending out signals to warn the bat that it is about to land a terrible-tasting meal. Several other types of moths are also able to detect the bat's sonar and avoid getting eaten.

Others use scare tactics to get away . . .

The **frilled lizard** scares off predators by rearing up and unfolding its fierce-looking frill. With its frill down, the lizard looks like the bark that it sits on, and it is hard to spot. When a predator comes near,

the lizard will first crouch down against the bark. If the predator continues, the lizard will rear up, open its mouth, and display its imposing frill. Sometimes it will hiss and jump forward to add to the frightening effect.

Who Am I?

I charge my prey at such great speeds they usually don't have a chance to escape. I am so ferocious, I've even been known to devour humans.

Am I . . .

a. a gorilla?
b. an elephant?
c. a komodo dragon?
d. a buffalo ?

Some creatures have bodyguards . . .

On their shells, **hermit crabs** carry anemones, whose stinging tentacles protect them from predators. When the crab moves to a new shell, sometimes the anemone does, too. In the wild, hermit crabs eat plants and other animals. Some people keep the land-dwelling species of hermit crab as pets.

Some use trickery . . .

The **California roadrunner** captures rattlesnakes by piling cactus spines around the snakes while they sleep. This desert bird, native to South America, Mexico, and the southwestern United States, is the state bird of New Mexico. When it runs, it raises its tail and lowers its head so that they are level with the horizon.

The **crested bellbird** fools predators by moving its voice from tree to tree like a ventriloquist. Bellbirds are found in wetland areas of Australia and in Venezuela.

The songs and cries of the **lyrebird** are imitations of other birds. This bird lives deep in the forests of Australia.

Some critters throw up . . .

When attacked, the **sea cucumber** defends itself by expelling its own digestive system. The attacker becomes entangled in it, and the sea cucumber goes free. Luckily, the sea cucumber, which lives on the seafloor, is able to regenerate its insides.

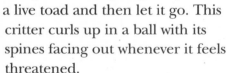

Some make foam . . .

The **hedgehog** eats poisonous toads, then froths at the mouth and licks toad toxins onto its spines to protect itself from predators. Sometimes, though, the hedgehog will just lick a live toad and then let it go. This critter curls up in a ball with its spines facing out whenever it feels threatened.

Who Am I?

Don't mess with me. I can secrete enough venom to kill seven people.

Am I a type of . . .

a. horned toad?
b. boa constrictor?
c. blowfish?
d. octopus?

Others make noise. . .

The roar of the **tiger** can be heard for a distance of two miles. This Asian cat is the largest member of the cat family, so it's not so surprising that its voice can carry. The average weight of a tiger is between 500 and 600 pounds. The largest tiger ever recorded was a male Siberian tiger that weighed in at 1,025 pounds!

And some power spray . . .

The **civet**, a catlike animal found in Africa and Asia, drives off its enemies with a foul-smelling spray. This spray is actually used in the manufacture of some perfumes. Pee-yew!

When pursued by a hawk, the **houbara bustard** sprays its foe's eyes and feathers with a thick sticky fluid that blinds and disables it. This desert bird was once common on the Arabian Peninsula and across Central Asia and Pakistan, but because of overhunting, the houbara bustard has become endangered.

Some creatures squirt blood . . .

The **horned toad** reacts to attack by squirting blood from its eyes as far as four feet. This lizard, the official state reptile of Texas, can measure up to five inches long. Its horns are actually scales on the sides and back of its head. When threatened, the horned toad will first flatten itself in hopes of not being seen. Then it will puff its body up to twice its normal size. Finally, the lizard will resort to its blood-squirting trick. It can squirt blood both forward and backward.

Who Am I?

Even after I have died, I can still slash and bite an attacker.

Am I . . .

a. an alligator?
b. a caiman?
c. a wolf?
d. a bobcat?

Stand on their heads . . .

The **stickleback** fish frightens off predators by standing on its head. There are a number of different kinds of sticklebacks. Some live in freshwater, some live in salt water, and some live in brackish waters, which are a mix of salt and fresh. The stickleback get its name from the spines on its back. Some people think sticklebacks may be killing off native fish in parts of the United States by eating their eggs.

Or wear protective gear . . .

The **sponge crab** cuts a piece of sponge and fits it perfectly over its back to make itself unappetizing to predators. This crab holds its sponge in place with its back pair of legs. Often sponge crabs also wear a coating of algae, which gives them further protection from the octopuses that like to eat them. If a sponge crab can't find a piece of sponge, it will use a piece of shell, a sea anemone, or even part of a tourist's flip-flop sandal.

The **porcupine** puffs up its quills, which makes it look quite unappetizing. If attacked, the porcupine will use its tail to drive the quills into its foe. Porcupine quills are

painful and are hard to remove. The quills have barbs (little hooks) that point backward and tear the skin if you try to pull them out.

Some critters wear a disguise . . .

Large, thorny spines cover the body and tail of the **thorny devil**, helping it blend into its harsh desert home. The favorite food of this Australian lizard is ants, which it licks up one at a time with its sticky tongue.

Who Am I?

It would be hard for a predator to sneak up on me. That's because my eyes move independently of each other so I can look in two directions at the same time.

Am I . . .

a. a chameleon?
b. an owl?
c. a bat?
d. a hawk?

The **measuring worm**, which is actually the caterpillar of a moth, deceives predators with its camouflage. Its colors help it to blend in with the twigs of trees on which it feeds. Some types of measuring worms have little spikes that stick up and look just like tiny twigs. This caterpillar can also stand on one end and remain motionless. That way it looks even more like part of the tree.

Some join gangs . . .

Meerkats join together to fight a predator. They stand on their hind legs and move forward menacingly as if they were one fierce animal. When working with their gang—the name for a group of meerkats—they can scare off some of their major predators, including jackals and cobras.

Show off their high jumps . . .

Gazelles can leap high into the air to show a predator that it has been spotted and to try and discourage it from pursuit. This kind of jumping—straight up into the air—is known as "pronking."

Or simply kick . . .

An **ostrich** can kill a lion with one well-placed kick. This flightless bird is the largest bird in the world, and can grow up to eight feet tall, weigh 300 pounds, and run more than 40 miles per hour.

Some animals go undercover . . .

The **yellow-footed marsupial mouse**, which is also known as an antechinus, escapes the notice of flying predators by walking upside

down on a twig. Like other marsupials, the mother gives birth to tiny babies that live inside her pouch until they are big enough to move around on their own.

Spit stunning poison . . .

The **spitting cobra** of Africa can spray venom through an opening in the front of its fangs for several feet. Its venom can cause blindness.

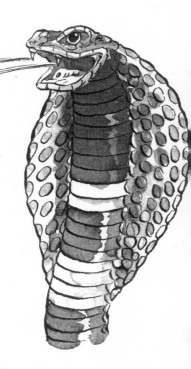

Show their sharp teeth . . .

The **wolf fish**, has so vicious a bite that its teeth can leave marks on an iron anchor. Despite its fearsome jaws, these fish spend much of their time hiding among the rocks on the seafloor.

Curl into a ball . . .

When threatened, the **pangolin**, which is also known as the spiny anteater, rolls itself up so tightly that three men pulling at its tail cannot straighten it out. The name "pangolin" comes from the Malay word that means "to roll."

Who Am I?

Other animals can tell how fierce I am by the length of my beard.

Am I . . .

a. an antelope?
b. a goat?
c. a bison?
d. a bull?

Do their best to hide . . .

The **solenodon** buries its head in the sand to escape detection by a predator. This ratlike, insect-eating creature is very rare. Found only in Haiti and Cuba, the nocturnal solenodon, a relative of moles and hedgehogs, lives in dense, humid forests and on the edges of plantations. Some scientists estimate that there may be fewer than 100 left in existence.

Develop magnificent eyesight . . .

The **giraffe**'s eyes protrude so far it can see in all directions without turning its head. This panoramic view allows it to spot a predator approaching from any direction. The giraffe's acute vision also lets it communicate through body language with other giraffes standing far away.

Or simply fall apart . . .

The **starfish** snaps off all its arms when frightened. Luckily, it is capable of regeneration. It grows new arms when it loses the old ones. In some cases, if a large piece breaks off a starfish, it can grow into a whole new creature.

Who Am I?

I am known for my terrible temper and will quickly charge anything that disturbs me. But if I am captured, I am easily tamed and become gentle and affectionate.

Am I . . .

a. a tiger?
b. a lion?
c. a polar bear?
d. a rhinoceros?

Friends or foes? Animals and people can be the best of friends or the worst of enemies. This Brain Buster is filled with off-the-wall info about amazing rescues. One astounding tale is complete hogwash. Are you up to the challenge of figuring out which one?

a. In 1938, 60 beaver colonies saved major highways, bridges, and hundreds of acres of valuable land in Stony Point, New York, from a raging flood. How'd they do it? By doing what beavers do best—they built dams that measured up to 600 feet long and 14 feet wide.

Believe It!   Not!

b. Monkeys took care of two-year-old John Ssebunya after he got lost in the jungle. The monkeys taught him to survive on fruits, nuts, and berries. After four years, John was found living among the monkeys and returned to his village in Uganda.

Believe It!   Not!

c. Lulu, a pig from Beaver Falls, Pennsylvania, saved the life of her owner. When Jo Altsaman suffered a massive heart attack, Lulu squeezed through the doggie door and ran into the road where she lay down and played dead. She got the attention of a young man whom she then led to Altsaman. He called 911, and Altsaman made it to the hospital in time for doctors to save her life!

Believe It!   Not!

337

d. Rats have an uncanny ability to find food. In 1993, a 14-year-old girl who was trapped on a deserted island in Indonesia was able to survive for three weeks on food she scavenged by following these rodents.

Believe It!   Not!

• •

BONUS QUESTION

What happened in 1891 when a sperm whale swallowed James Bartley?

a. Yuck! The whale spat him right back out. Bartley sustained only minor injuries and went on to become a renowned harpooner.

b. There were so many living fish swimming inside the whale's stomach that Bartley was able to survive for 42 days by using them for food.

c. The whale was badly injured by harpoons, and the next day, it was found dead, floating on the surface. Bartley was found in the whale's stomach, unconscious but still breathing.

Some mothers have lots of young at once . . .

The **nine-banded armadillo** always gives birth to quadruplets of the same sex. The babies are identical and are all formed from a single egg. The armadillo is the only mammal that regularly produces multiple young from one egg. Originally native to South America, this creature can now be found in Kansas, Louisiana, Oklahoma, and Texas.

The **tailless tenrec**, which is also known as the Madagascar hedgehog, regularly produces the largest litters of any mammal—as many as 32 babies at once. When threatened, a tenrec baby rubs together the bristles on its back. This produces an audible alarm signal that alerts its mother to the danger.

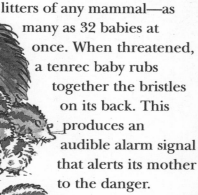

Others usually have one at a time . . .

A newborn **kangaroo** is typically just one inch long. Immediately after birth, this tiny blind creature crawls into its mother's pouch to nurse. Kangaroo mothers actually produce two different kinds of milk, allowing both newborn joeys (baby kangaroos) and an older sibling to nurse at the same time.

A newborn **panda** weighs just three to five ounces, about 1/900 of its mother's weight. Blind and hairless, the infant panda is constantly held and cradled by its mother for a week or more.

Who Am I?

My legs are as long at birth as they will be when I grow up.

Am I . . .

a. a horse?
b. a cat?
c. a koala?
d. a raccoon?

A **blue whale** infant gains weight at the rate of eight to ten pounds an hour. That's roughly 200 pounds or more a day! A newborn blue whale calf weighs about three tons and measures 23 to 27 feet long.

Some moms would do anything for their babies . . .

When a young **herring gull** taps the red mark on its mother's beak, she throws up whatever she has just eaten to feed it. Herring gulls will eat just about anything, from clams to dead animals to French fries. Some even scavenge food from garbage dumps, rather than looking for food at the seashore.

To make a soft, cozy home for its babies, the **white-eared honey-eater** steals the hair from passersby to line its nest. This songbird possesses a long, forked, tubular tongue. To feed, it sticks its tongue into flowers and sucks out the nectar and any small insects hiding inside.

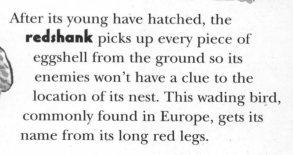

After its young have hatched, the **redshank** picks up every piece of eggshell from the ground so its enemies won't have a clue to the location of its nest. This wading bird, commonly found in Europe, gets its name from its long red legs.

The **golden eagle** attacks anything that approaches its nest—even helicopters and airplanes. This eagle lives in the mountains of Asia, Europe, and North America. Using sticks, it builds its nest in a tree or on a cliff. Every year, the golden eagle returns to the same nest to lay its eggs.

Who Am I?

After I produce my young, I often change my gender from male to female.

Am I . . .

a. a swordfish?
b. a crab?
c. a lobster?
d. an oyster?

An **octopus** protects her brood by starving herself. She stays with her eggs instead of looking for food. Most species of octopus lay their eggs in grapelike clusters, which they protect with their arms. The octopus is found in nearly all the oceans of the world.

And others would do anything to them . . .

The **water shrew** devours her babies if they don't follow her instructions. Some species of water shrew bear up to three litters a year, each one consisting of four to eight blind, hairless babies.

Some fathers care for their young . . .

At night, the male **ostrich** risks his life guarding his nest—even fighting lions to protect his newborn chicks. One male usually lives with a flock of three to five females, who lay their eggs in one communal nest. The nest can hold from 15 to 60 eggs. During the day, the females take turns watching the eggs.

Male **gorillas** band together to defend their young from poachers. Gorillas typically live in groups of five to ten individuals in the dense forests of central Africa. Full-grown adult males can weigh as much as 400 pounds and stand as tall as six feet. Mature males are called "silverback" gorillas after the wide band of silvery fur on their back.

The **sand grouse** flies as far as 50 miles a day to soak himself in water so that his young can drink from his feathers. A relative of the pigeon, the sand grouse lives in desert areas of Africa and Asia. When there are eggs in the nest, the grouse

stays with them all day long to shade them from the hot sun. Once the chicks are hatched, the male heads to the nearest waterhole. He does this until his offspring are big enough to visit the waterhole themselves.

Who Am I?

I'm such a good father, I always hatch and feed my young.

Am I . . .

a. a crocodile?
b. a snake?
c. a platypus?
d. an emu?

The male **Darwin frog** hatches eggs in a pouch in his mouth. The female lays about 30 eggs on land, and the male guards them for two weeks before picking them up in his mouth. When the tadpoles lose their tails and become tiny frogs, they jump out of Daddy's mouth. Native to South America, this frog gets its name from Charles Darwin, the great naturalist who described their strange habits in the late 19th century. In Argentina, the Darwin frog is also known as a "vaquero."

Some parents feed their babies all day . . .

In searching for food, the **house wren** makes as many as 12,000 flights from its nest in a single day. This little songbird lays five to eight eggs in a clutch (or group) and can bear up to two clutches a year. The house wren will nest in birdhouses, trees—even in the pockets of clothes hung on a line to dry.

Some don't feed them at all . . .

The **cowbird** lays her eggs in the nests of other bird species and then takes off. Once the cowbird chick hatches, the other mother bird feeds the cowbird chick along with her own brood. Because of its behavior, the cowbird is known as a brood parasite.

Some parents take their babies everywhere . . .

Although a **pangolin** baby can walk a few days after birth, it rides on its mother's tail instead. If the mother feels threatened, she will curl her tail, with the baby on it, under her body. Any predators have to go through her before they can reach her baby.

The male **finfoot** carries his chicks in special pockets under his wings so he can fly with them. The finfoot is thought to be the only bird that carries its chicks in this way. Found in parts of Asia, Africa, Central and South America, these birds are also known as sun grebes.

Baby **wolf spiders** live on their mother's back until they are old enough to be on their own. This spider, which does not spin a web, also carries her eggs to protect them from predators.

And some leave them in daycare . . .

Who Am I?

I am three times longer than the egg I hatched from.

Am I . . .

a. an eagle chick?
b. a baby alligator?
c. an ostrich chick?
d. a cowbird chick?

Penguin parents leave their chicks in rookeries where they are watched over by other adult penguins. This allows both parents to go out looking for food. Penguins live only in the Southern Hemisphere.

Some babies take baths in mud . . .

A baby **elephant** takes mud baths to protect itself from sunburn. This also helps keep the animal cool and gets rid of pesky insects. Young elephants will often squirm around in the mud together and form a messy heap. Adults tend to pick the mud up with their trunks and fling it so that it lands on their bodies with a thwack.

And some are afraid to swim . . .

When it gets old enough, a baby **seal** gets pushed into the water by its mother, who stays beside it until it loses its fear of the water. Newborn seals have a soft, downy coat that absorbs water. As they grow up, the young seals shed that coat and grow water-repellent fur. At that point, the young seals must learn to swim so they can hunt for food and escape from predators such as killer whales, polar bears, and sharks.

Some babies really stick together . . .

Baby **eels** travel in such tight formation, they often look like a ball of yarn. Some species of eel live in the ocean. Others inhabit freshwater. Some freshwater eels swim to the sea to lay their eggs. The eggs hatch and the eel larvae emerge. They grow and become elvers. The elvers eventually swim back to freshwater. Often they can be found in large groups at the mouths of rivers and streams.

Who Am I?

When I am a newborn, I leave no scent, so predators don't have a clue that I'm nearby.

Am I . . .

a. a skunk?
b. a tortoise?
c. a ferret?
d. a deer?

While others take up the whole nest . . .

Cuckoos, like cowbirds, are considered brood parasites. The mother cuckoo lays its egg in the nest of another bird species and leaves it to be hatched by the foster family. Sometimes the young cuckoo is bigger than its foster mother as well as its foster siblings. It competes with these siblings for food and may even push them out of the nest.

Ready to tackle the truth? You know the drill. Go for it!

a. Adult geese are highly protective of their goslings. When seven-year-old Megan Waltz of Newark, Delaware, hugged a young goose, a gaggle of geese held her captive in a tree for over 26 hours before firefighters were able to rescue her.

Believe It!   **Not!**

b. A cat, owned by A.W. Mitchell of Vancouver, British Columbia, nurtured 25 baby chicks.

Believe It!   **Not!**

c. A Canada goose and a Siberian husky from a farm in Yakima, Washington, are BFFs—best friends forever. Not only does the goose sleep in the doghouse and share the dog's food, but it will face off against other dogs that try to enter the doghouse.

Believe It!   **Not!**

d. Golden Duke, a rooster owned by O.J. Plomeson of Luverne, Minnesota, could pull Plomeson's baby daughter in a carriage down Main Street!

Believe It!   **Not!**

BONUS QUESTION

What made Koko, a gorilla who understands the meaning of at least 500 words in sign language, cry for two days?

a. She was told that her pet cat had died.

b. She was told she had to move to another zoo.

c. She realized two young boys were using sign language to insult her.

d. She was bullied by an older and bigger gorilla.

POP QUIZ

It's not over yet. How much do you remember about World's Weirdest Critters? It's time to test your knowledge. Ready to tackle the toughest Ripley's Brain Buster yet? Circle your answers and give yourself five points for each question you answer correctly.

1. Which one of the following is NOT something animals do with their tongues?
a. Suck nectar from flowers.
b. Catch ants.
c. Clean the lint out of their navels.

2. Hippo sweat looks like blood, but it's really . . .
a. a kind of skin conditioner.
b. a mucouslike coating that protects hippos from poisonous plants.
c. a slime that makes it difficult for predators to attack them.  The hippos are so slippery, attackers hit their sides and slide right off.

3. If a crocodile loses a tooth, it just grows back. It can lose and regrow up to 300 teeth in its lifetime.

Believe It!   **Not!**

4. The ruffed grouse grows wings every year right before winter so it can fly south.

Believe It!   **Not!**

5. Which oddity is false?

a. The cormorant can eat three times its weight in fish each day.

b. A bat can eat over 3,000 insects in one night.

c. A Siberian brown bear will only eat fish heads.

d. A hummingbird drinks the nectar from 1,000 flowers every day.

6. Which one don't you believe?

a. A polar bear can smell its prey up to 100 miles away.

b. A coyote can hear a mouse moving under one foot of snow.

c. The green-backed heron catches insects and uses them as bait to lure fish.

d. The trapdoor spider builds a burrow with a trapdoor and waits for dinner to drop by.

7. What does a hummingbird use to build its nest?
a. The stems of dead flowers.
b. Spiderwebs.
c. Anything it can find—including straw, weeds, and even garbage.

8. Which one is NOT a way that animals help one another?
a. Birds pick and clean the teeth of crocodiles.
b. Birds eat ticks off a rhino's back.
c. Birds balance vertically on water while schools of small fish remove dirt from their feathers.

9. Which is NOT a way that animals communicate with one another?
a. A language of sounds similar to Japanese.
b. Dancing.
c. Low-frequency sounds.
d. Electrical signals.

10. Flying dragons can glide up to 150 feet!

Believe It! **Not!**

11. Prairie dogs identify one another by kissing. They press their teeth against one another's faces.

Believe It! **Not!**

12. Which is false?

a. Some moths are able to jam a bat's sonar so the bat can't find them.

b. The California roadrunner captures snakes by luring them into a pit using a trail of cactus spines.

c. The lyrebird can impersonate the songs and cries of other birds.

d. The sea cucumber defends itself by "throwing up" its own digestive system.

13. What does the houbara bustard do when it's being chased by a hawk?

a. Sprays the hawk's eyes and feathers with a thick sticky fluid that blinds and disables it.

b. Retaliates with a foul-smelling spray.

c. Squirts blood from its eyes.

d. Curls up into a ball.

14. A female octopus protects her brood by hiding them inside conch shells.

Believe It!   **Not!**

15. Baby seals have to be taught not to be afraid of the water.

Believe It!   **Not!**

Answer Key

Chapter One

Who Am I?
Page 282:   **d.** turtle
Page 284:   **a.** Manx
Page 286:   **b.** squirrel
Page 288:   **c.** earthworm
Page 291:   **c.** lobster
Page 292:   **d.** platypus
Brain Buster: **c** is false.
Bonus Question: a.

Chapter Two

Who Am I?
Page 296:   **a.** parrot
Page 299:   **d.** pelican eel
Page 300:   **b.** fish (Indian climbing perch)
Page 302   **b.** crab
Page 304:   **c.** oyster
Page 306:   **a.** giant panda
Brain Buster: **b** is false.
Bonus Question: c.

Chapter Three

Who Am I?

Page 310:   **b.** mockingbird
Page 312:   **a.** ant (magnetic ant)
Page 314:   **c.** ant (Amazon ant)
Page 316:   **d.** owl (burrowing owl)
Brain Buster: c is false.
Bonus Question: b.

Chapter Four

Who Am I?

Page 320:   **b.** sheep
Page 322:   **d.** monkey (Barbary macaque)
Page 325:   **a.** cowbird
Page 326:   **c.** komodo dragon
Page 328:   **d.** octopus (blue-ringed octopus)
Page 330:   **b.** caiman
Page 332:   **a.** chameleon
Page 335:   **c.** bison
Page 336:   **d.** rhinoceros
Brain Buster: d is false.
Bonus Question: c.

Chapter Five

Who Am I?

Page 340: **a.** horse

Page 342: **d.** oyster

Page 344: **d.** emu

Page 346: **b.** baby alligator

Page 348: **d.** deer

Brain Buster: a is false.

Bonus Question: a.

Pop Quiz

1. **c.**
2. **a.**
3. **Believe It!**
4. **Not!**
5. **a.**
6. **a.**
7. **b.**
8. **c.**
9. **a.**
10. **Believe It!**
11. **Believe It!**
12. **b.**
13. **a.**
14. **Not!**
15. **Believe It!**

What's Your Ripley's Rank?

Ripley's Scorecard

Congrats! Now it's time to rate your Ripley's knowledge. Are you an Extreme Expert or a Ripley's Rookie? Check out the answers in the answer key and use this page to keep track of how many trivia questions you've answered correctly. Then add 'em up and find out how you rate.

Here's the scoring breakdown—give yourself:
★ **10 points** for every **Who Am I?** you answered correctly;

★ **20 points** for every fiction you spotted in the **Ripley's Brain Busters**;

★ **10** for every **Bonus Question** you answered right and;

★ **5** for every **Pop Quiz** question you answered correctly.

Here's a tally sheet:
Number of **Who Am I?** questions
answered correctly: _____ x 10 = _____

Number of **Ripley's Brain Busters**
questions answered correctly: _____ x 20 = _____

Number of **Bonus Questions**
answered correctly: _____ x 10 = _____

Chapter Total: _____

Write your totals for each chapter and the Pop Quiz
section in the spaces below. Then add them up to get
your FINAL SCORE. Your FINAL SCORE decides
how you rate.

Chapter One Total: _____

Chapter Two Total: _____

Chapter Three Total _____

Chapter Four Total: _____

Chapter Five Total: _____

Pop Quiz Total: _____

FINAL SCORE: _____

525—301
Extreme Expert

Your Ripley's know-how is top-notch. No one can pull
anything over on you. You just don't fall for tricks. You
know that truth can be stranger than fiction—and you
like it that way. Your sense for the strange, bent for the
bizarre, and talent for spotting the truth in the absurd
are hard to believe. And you wow your friends with your
grasp of the freakish and outlandish. Maybe you have
discovered a rare Ripley's oddity of your own—or maybe
it's time to add yourself to the ranks of the truly
amazing. You're superhuman—**Believe It!**

300–201
Best of the Bizarre

Your Ripley's know-how ranks high. You have an impressive eye for the bizarre, but you're no know-it-all. Your ability to spot a hoax is uncanny, but even the best get stumped once in a while. Cut yourself some slack—the line between truth and fiction isn't always so easy to figure out. Trust your instincts—and keep it up, superstar!

200–101
Amazing Amateur

You're rising in the ranks, but tales of sea cucumbers throwing up their insides are more than you can deal with. You can separate the more obvious fictions from the facts, but when it comes to the Brain Busters, your sense for the strange is out of whack. Chin up! Give it another try—you've got shocking potential.

100–0
Ripley's Rookie

The odd, bizarre, and super-strange are just not your style. It's too much to think about. You'd prefer to strain your brain on less amazing tales. You stick to the everyday, the concrete, the norm—and you're not apologizing for it. That's cool. But remember, the world is a weird and wacky place. And sometimes the truth really is stranger than fiction.

Photo Credits

Ripley Entertainment and the editors of this book wish to thank the following photographers, agents, and other individuals for permission to use and reprint the following photographs in this book. Any photographs included in this book that are not acknowledged below are property of the Ripley Archives. Great effort has been made to obtain permission from the owners of all materials included in this book. Any errors that may have been made are unintentional and will gladly be corrected in future printings if notice is sent to Ripley Entertainment, 5728 Major Boulevard, Orlando, Florida 32819.

281 Anteater; 283 Wolf; 284 Sphynx; 287 Walrus;
295 Bat, Pheasant; 298 Koala; 304 Sea Snake;
303 Polar Bear; 306 Moray Eel;
310 Hummingbird; 315 Hermit Crab;
323 Gorilla; 324 Cranes; 326 Frilled Lizard;
328 Sea Cucumber; 329 Tiger; 331 Porcupine;
333 Meerkats; 336 Giraffe; 340 Kangaroos;
345 House Wren; 346 Penguins; 347 Baby
Elephant/Copyright © 2001 Ripley
Entertainment and its licensors

282 Tuatara/Steven Holt/Aigrette Stockpix

292 Aardvark; 299 Peregrine Falcon;
336 Starfish/PhotoDisc

297 Hummingbird; 342 Octopus/CORBIS

301 Elephant Seals/Dennis Sheridan

302 Osprey; 309 Lion/EyeWire

305 Trapdoor Spider; 312 Water Spider/David
Glynne Fox

321 Red-capped Mangabey/Samantha Smith/
Yerkes Regional Primate Research Center

322 Prairie Dogs/W. Perry/CORBIS

327 Crested Bellbird/Kevin Roberts

332 Thorny Devil/Gerry Ellis/Minden
Pictures

334 Marsupial Mouse/John Eisenberg

344 Sand Grouse/Keith Sloan/Nature Portfolio